T0383838

Health Care in the Next Curve

Health Care in the Next Curve

Transforming a Dysfunctional Industry

John Abendshien

Routledge
Taylor & Francis Group

A PRODUCTIVITY PRESS BOOK

Routledge
Taylor & Francis Group
711 Third Avenue, New York, NY 10017

© 2019 by Taylor & Francis Group, LLC
Productivity Press is an imprint of Taylor & Francis Group, an Informa business

No claim to original U.S. Government works

Printed on acid-free paper

International Standard Book Number-13: 978-1-1386-2654-6 (Hardback)
International Standard Book Number-13: 978-1-3152-2813-6 (ebook)

Library of Congress Cataloging-in-Publication Data

Names: Abendshien, John, author.
Title: Health care in the next curve : transforming a dysfunctional industry / John Abendshien.
Description: Boca Raton : Taylor & Francis, 2018. | Includes bibliographical references.
Identifiers: LCCN 2018009308 | ISBN 9781138626546 (hardback : alk. paper) | ISBN 9781315228136 (ebook)
Subjects: | MESH: Health Care Sector--economics | Economics, Medical | Health Care Sector--trends | Insurance, Health--economics | Delivery of Health Care--economics | United States
Classification: LCC RA410.53 | NLM W 74 AA1 | DDC 338.4/73621--dc23
LC record available at https://lccn.loc.gov/2018009308

Visit the Taylor & Francis Web site at
http://www.taylorandfrancis.com

and the Productivity Press Web site at
http://www.ProductivityPress.com

Contents

Foreword

Truly understanding the complexity of American health care requires an individual who has been immersed in it for many years. It must be someone who has worked in different kinds of systems in different parts of the country. It must be someone who has studied policy and who understands operations and the multiple components of the delivery system. John Abendshien is one of those rare individuals who has done all of that. His extensive experience, as it relates to his knowledge of a wide variety of health care providers and technologies, has been distilled into this important book.

I have known John and used his expertise for 30 years while working in senior health care executive roles, including serving as CEO of two hospitals in Colorado and a six-hospital system in California. In those roles, I relied upon his strategic mind to help guide the organizations I led. John has a unique combination of intelligence and compassion that enables him to evaluate the big picture of health care and then bring it into focus at the local level. I have benefitted from his wisdom on both a professional and personal level. He is a diligent student who can synthesize huge pieces of data to develop practical and yet innovative plans. Beyond that, he is a remarkable human being who cares about people and the industry he has devoted his life to improving.

John notes in Chapter 1 that, as of yet, there is no fix for American health care, as it remains burdened with high costs and less-than-stellar outcomes. He reminds us that lack of progress is not because people have not been trying to improve things. Unfortunately, most efforts have not attacked the underlying factors behind the complexity and fragmentation in today's health care system. Thus, in chapters 2–7 he lays out five core causes for the system issues we currently face.

Fortunately, John does not leave us there. Instead, he describes a blueprint for transformative change that is not a government-run solution. With an optimistic and inspiring voice, he describes the unleashing of the "economic human" who is equipped with the Big Data that will enable individuals to make their own health care decisions. In this new future, what he describes as the "Next Curve," is an informed market that can make rational decisions when it comes to access, choice, and value in health care. John accurately points out that it is only recently that such Big Data exists in a way that can inform the market about the true costs of health care and the relative value of various delivery options.

Of course, there must be changes to empower people with that information. John suggests that five systemic changes must happen for such transformation: fixing the safety nets for those most in need; restructuring health insurance; realigning the reimbursement system; removing the barriers to care coordination; and finally, eliminating harmful or otherwise counterproductive regulations.

If the industry and an information-enabled market can effectively make these transformational changes, John convincingly describes a new future that would not be unlike the changes we have seen in the airline and telecommunication industries. Those examples give evidence that Americans can make rational decisions when they have real information that enables them to do so.

Over the past two years I worked on my doctoral dissertation to complete the requirements for my PhD from Claremont University. My research for the dissertation included interviewing 40 executive and physician leaders in the industry.

I was sometimes disheartened by the interviews, as many of the individuals described their frustration and exhaustion from working in a fragmented system. These were outstanding people, working long hours to make the lives of patients better. But, they encountered what seemed like insurmountable issues that were out of their control. Several of them concluded that, while they did not like it, they were moving toward an acceptance that a government solution was inevitable. Others just wanted to retire. Excellent and affordable health care did not seem in the realm of possibility to them.

However, with his rich background and clarity of vision, John describes a hopeful and much better alternative. His belief in people, his understanding of economics, and his knowledge of the myriad of components that make up the complex American health care system have helped him seize the opportunity of following a different path—the Next Curve in American health care.

Preface

We are in what could accurately be described as the perfect storm of health care. The cost of medicine in the U.S. is high by any international measure, yet our health outcome indicators are low when compared with those of other industrialized countries. We are facing an unprecedented growth in demand for health care services. This is due in no small part to the aging of our society—the *silver tsunami*—but is also being driven by lifestyle behaviors and related morbidities in our younger population segments. All of this is generating strong upward pressures on the cost curve. But there's a limit to how much society is willing or able to pay for health care. When you put these factors together, we face a possible future where government-imposed rationing provisions will micromanage the business of medicine. In this scenario the government could determine who will receive health care, what resources will be made available, and how it will be delivered.

With each change in the political leadership in Washington, there's renewed hope that we might finally find some real solutions to the health care problems confronting the nation. This is a false hope. If anything, we should be grateful that the most recent legislative attempts to repeal and replace Obamacare came to an early demise. Washington is not especially famous for having well-engineered solutions to anything, let alone being able to fix what is arguably the most complex industry ecosystem on the planet.

Nor is the health care industry itself able to fix its ills. "Health care, heal thyself" is not a realistic proposition. One of the major reasons for this is the confluence of mutual interests on the part of provider industry insiders, insurance executives, and government bureaucrats. This panoply of interests, which I refer to as the medical-administrative complex—or "MAC" for short—is the primary reason why health care has become so bizarrely complicated and costly. In this book we'll personalize MAC because in so many ways he has taken on a life of his own. Suffice it to say that MAC doesn't want real solutions. So much of his livelihood is dependent on creating and perpetuating dysfunction—an industry ecology that involves bureaucratically driven changes, micro-managed oversight, and the need to *fix* the unintended consequences that MAC himself has created.

The current state of the industry can be directly or indirectly linked to five core systemic problems—what are referred to in this book as the root causes of industry dysfunction. These problems include a continued lack of affordable access for many citizens; an industry financing and insurance model that effectively insulates all the parties from the economic consequences of health care decisions; a provider payment model that rewards inefficiency and waste; a fragmented delivery structure that is problem-specific but that fails to take care of the whole person; and, finally, a regulatory structure that creates cost, complexity, and dysfunction at every turn. As is chronicled in this book, these root causes are the direct product of 100+ years of legislative and policy direction that has served MAC well. The rest of us, not so much.

The forces of change leading to true transformation will not come from the industry insiders or big government. They will come from the outside. They will come from the market itself. This book explores the concept of rational choice, which is the economic principle that informed people will select from among available options the solution that will give them the greatest value. The key words here are informed and value.

Historically, the market has lacked the objective, quantifiable information necessary to identify various health care options and weigh their relative value.

This has changed dramatically. With the exponential growth of Big Data and the rich abundance of its downstream technologies, the market now has objective, quantified information that it can use to compare both the effectiveness and cost of various health care products and services. What economists refer to as *the economic human* is now in a position to radically transform the industry landscape.

The futurist Ian Morrison defined the Second Curve of health care as one that is driven by value. This has been a positive dynamic in the evolution of the industry model over the past decade. But the ultimate potential of the Second Curve dynamic has been limited by existing regulatory and payment structures. As will be explored in detail in this book, those structures affect market and industry behaviors in ways that work against the very concept of value.

In the new future of health care, we need to unleash the economic human and allow an empowered market to make the needed transformational changes. This will require more *undoing* than *doing*, which is to say that we need to systematically go after the root causes of industry dysfunction, and eliminate or radically overhaul the outdated financing, delivery, and regulatory structures that exist today. With this transformation we can have a market-driven market with expanded safety nets, affordable access, and more consumer options. We can have a purchase and consumer market that is quantitatively informed, and that is able to make rational choices on the basis of measureable, comparable value. We can pave the way for a competitive market dynamic, with powerful incentives for continuous product improvement.

In this new future we can unleash the economic human. We can restore the spirit of medicine. This is the Next Curve of health care. Enjoy the ride.

Author

John Abendshien, President and co-founder of Integrated Clinical Solutions, Inc. (ICS), has over 40 years of experience providing consulting services to health care organizations in the areas of enterprise strategy, clinical service line development, organizational design, mergers and acquisitions, and network formation. He has conducted consulting engagements with a broad range of organizations across the United States, including health care systems, academic medical centers, physician groups, insurance companies and government agencies, as well as professional and trade organizations.

Over the course of his career John as interviewed and worked with literally thousands of health care professionals representing a broad cross-section of disciplines. He has been directly involved in the design of cutting-edge strategic solutions, and has guided the boardroom decision-making that has defined the priorities and direction of many leading health care organizations.

John is a frequent speaker and lecturer on the subject of strategic planning and organizational change management. He has written numerous journal articles on these and related topics, and is author of the book: *"A Board Guide to Strategic Business Planning"* (American Hospital Publishing, 1988). John also serves as Senior Health Care Advisor to The Chicago Corporation, a major Chicago-based investment-banking firm.

Prior to founding ICS, John was Partner and National Director of Ernst & Young LLP's health care strategy practice, with overall responsibility for that firm's health care strategy and mergers and acquisitions practice in the U.S. He also served as an officer in the U.S. Army Medical Services Corps.

John holds an MBA and an MS degree in Public Health from the University of Missouri-Columbia, and completed his administrative residency at the University of Washington Medical Center in Seattle, Washington.

INDUSTRY DYSFUNCTION: ITS ROOT CAUSES AND EFFECTS

I

1

INDUSTRY
DYSFUNCTION:
ITS ROOT CAUSES
AND EFFECTS

Chapter 1

It's Not the Future We Used to Have

"Life can only be understood backwards; but it must be lived forwards."

—**Søren Kierkegaard, 1813–1855**

CHAPTER OVERVIEW

- Political events have proven (once again) that we can't predict the future.
- The Second Curve of health care has moved us toward the concept of value, but we still haven't fixed the underlying, root causes of industry dysfunction.
- Much of what is wrong with health care can be linked directly to the roles and influence of government and industry stakeholders—a virtual medical-administrative complex of vested interests.

(Continued)

- We are now entering the Next Curve of health care, where an information-enabled market—the economic human—can make clinical, purchasing, and consumption decisions on the basis of measurable value.
- In the Next Curve this informed market is supplanting the medical-administrative complex as the driving force of change.

The Old Future

So much for my crystal ball. The initial outline of this book was in draft stages on that first Tuesday in November 2016. Like so many people, I fully expected that Hillary Clinton was about to make the move to the White House. Not only that, but I had some fairly well-developed notions about what the next few years would bring. We would, I thought, see an agenda of targeted tweaks to the Affordable Care Act (ACA, Obamacare). These would involve boosting enrollment, additional subsidies to consumers, tougher cost controls, and continued delivery system reforms. And then on to a public plan option. This would be the prototype for the later roll-out of a universal care model.

Early in my career, an economics professor warned me that if we live by the crystal ball, we must learn to eat ground glass. With the election of Donald J. Trump as President, I have found out what that ground glass tastes like. The world we thought we knew has not headed in the direction we thought it would go. As that well-known philosopher Yogi Berra famously said, "The future just ain't what it used to be."

There's still no health care fix in sight. As this book goes to press we don't have national legislation in place that will be the sequel to Obamacare. Elimination of the individual mandate notwithstanding, there's been no repeal. And, so far, no replacement.

Many believe that the results of the past presidential election sent a loud message that the country is not in favor of a stronger government role in health care. They point out that the Affordable Care Act took the whole idea of government-engineered health care out of the academic laboratory and put it to a real world test, and that it failed that test. That it fell far short of its original intention of ensuring access to health care for all. And worse, that it distorted the market in ways that led to skyrocketing insurance premiums, rising deductibles, and greatly diminished competition among health plans and providers.

But many others remain convinced that the real problem with the ACA is that the government didn't go far enough. They believe that what we need to do now is to move forward with a universal, single-payer model. Medicare for all. Many see this as a means of ensuring access for everyone, while providing the necessary controls over cost, quality, and safety.

Albert Einstein himself wasn't sure if he said it or not, but is widely credited with the definition of insanity as "doing the same thing over and over and expecting a different result." The problems of health care—access, cost, overutilization, and waste—didn't start with Obamacare. The legislative fixes that have been proposed to date would not only fail to remedy these problems, but would in many respects make them even more entrenched. We've had a long history of self-perpetuating prescription fails when it comes to health care: Attack the symptoms. Ignore the underlying pathology. Pass more laws. Create new, more complex problems. Hire more bureaucrats. Add regulations. Repeat the above as necessary.

Someday as we stand and look back at what happened (or didn't happen) in the early part of the Trump presidency, we may be grateful that we didn't have a quick repeal and replace scenario. As we'll explore in the chapters to come, the last thing we need is yet another academically designed, legislatively driven *reform* solution to our health care problems. Instead, we should take full advantage of this period of policy limbo to step back and take an objective, systematic look at the industry: its current state, how we got here, and a shared vision for a new future.

Regardless of the position that any of us may hold on this topic, I believe that we can all agree on one thing. Health care will be a centerpiece of national debate in the next election cycle. The country is still at a crossroad when it comes to the future direction of this industry. This realization has energized both the timing and direction of this book.

The Curves of Health Care

In his 1995 book, *The Second Curve*, the futurist Ian Morrison set forth the concept that companies can often get stuck in a *first curve* of a legacy model that is based on an earlier market state. He made the point that in order to survive and prosper, corporations must revamp their business models to respond to new market conditions, changing customer expectations, and new technologies. He referred to this new state as the Second Curve.[1]

Mr. Morrison then began to apply these same principles to health care. He described the industry First Curve as being essentially a volume-driven, cottage industry model, with largely independent caregivers who were paid on a fee-for-service basis. This curve, as we all know, led to uncontrolled costs, with little provider accountability for either clinical outcomes or economic performance. He went on to describe the Second Curve as being driven by the concept of *value*, with providers paid on the basis of reimbursement formulas that measure efficiency and quality.

I had the privilege of meeting with Mr. Morrison in the early days of his venture into the health care business. I was pleased to learn that we shared the principle that the creation and continuous enhancement of value was the common strategic denominator for any successful health care organization. Although we hadn't put the *curve* label on it, this was the core philosophy that had been driving my own firm's overall approach to developing positioning strategies for health systems throughout the country.

On a parallel track, numerous industry leaders have strongly supported the transition to a value-driven industry model. Michael Porter of the Harvard Business School, for example, has conducted industry-leading research on the concept of value in health care. He has stressed the importance of centering services on the needs of the patient, developing centers of excellence, coordinating care, ensuring geographic access, and focusing on measurable results.[2]

Over time, the health care industry has formally embraced the concept of the Second Curve and its emphasis on value. The American Hospital Association (AHA) has made it a guiding direction for its institutional members, with the core themes of value-based reimbursement, care coordination, and population health improvement.[3] This direction is also embodied in the Institute for Healthcare Improvement's *Triple Aim* objectives: improving the patient experience and the health of populations, while reducing the per capita cost of health care.[4] Without question the principles of the Second Curve and its focus on value have had a highly positive impact on the industry and the public it serves.

The Root Causes of Industry Dysfunction

In his initial description of the Second Curve phenomenon, Mr. Morrison warned us about the pitfalls of getting stuck in the same curve. His particular reference was to the First Curve, but this wise caution holds true for the Second Curve as well.

Despite its arguably positive impacts, the Second Curve has built-in roadblocks. These obstacles link directly to certain underlying, structural defects of the industry—the root causes of industry dysfunction. In fact, the preponderance of issues

1. Inadequate safety nets	• Many still without coverage or affordable access • Economic dislocations across rest of industry
2. Insurance model design	• Spiraling premium costs and deductibles • Lack of competitive products and consumer choice
3. Payment methodologies	• Overutilization, waste • High administrative overhead
4. Service fragmentation	• Lack of patient-centered care coordination • Poorly-designed care pathways, transitions
5. Regulatory dysfunction	• Inflated cost and pricing of care • Barriers to competition and innovation

Figure 1.1   Industry dysfunction: Root causes and effects.

that we face in health care today have either been created, or made worse by the following five core problems (Figure 1.1):

1. *Poorly-designed safety nets*: Some would argue that this is more of an effect than a cause. But it runs both ways. This is an ongoing policy fail that has consequences across the board. On the one hand we still have the reality—even with the ACA exchanges and Medicaid expansions—of a significant number of Americans who don't have affordable access to health care. And many others who are exposed to the consequences of catastrophic illness or injury. At the same time, our past fumbled attempts to deal with this problem have resulted in economic and functional dislo-cations that have had negative consequences for both the industry and the public served.

2. *Insurance that isn't really insurance anymore*: People have come to expect their health plan to cover any and all health-related expenses, including those generated by predictable care and services. For many, there's little economic consequence for decisions made regarding medical care. Under Obamacare, we have mandated, one-size-fits-all health plans (*essential benefits*) that give

consumers little choice in the way of products. All of this has made insurance too costly for many, especially younger people who would otherwise be able to afford basic coverage. And then there are the built-in inequities that give employee group plans a tax advantage that the rest of the population doesn't have.

3. *Payment methodologies that reward production*: Although there's been a much-needed movement toward more value-based payment approaches, most health care is still purchased on a traditional fee-for-service basis. Existing reimbursement methodologies, whether private or government, mostly pay caregivers for doing discrete things. This is as opposed to being accountable for the outcomes and costs associated with all services related to a given treatment or condition. All parties to the health transaction—consumers, providers, insurers, and regulators—are largely insulated from the economic consequences of the medical decisions that are made. The net result of all of this: service overutilization, waste, and an overall lack of care coordination.

4. *Service fragmentation across stages and levels of delivery*: Largely because of the way providers are paid, health care is structured around defined services, caregivers, and facilities. Not around patients, and not around their diseases and conditions. It's an industry of silos. There's an overall lack of inter-disciplinary and inter-institutional care coordination. Patients find it difficult and confusing to navigate through the care process. There's often little transition planning or continuity in ongoing recovery and condition management processes after the initial intervention has occurred. Information systems still don't talk to one another.

5. *Dysfunctional regulations*: Compliance requirements restrict the flexibility of caregivers to provide optimal treatment approaches. They impose unnecessary layers of administrative overhead and costs. Government price-setting

has resulted in sub-optimal services and higher costs. Certificate of Need laws limit competition and restrict the ability of health care systems to make rational resource allocations. Regulations suppress innovation. Existing tort laws make medicine more expensive for everyone.

The current state of our health care industry didn't just happen. The root causes cited above have in large measure been created and perpetuated by our political and regulatory structures, and by a virtual sub-industry of bureaucrats and administrators. These structures reside within the ranks of government agencies, insurers, health systems, trade associations, and outside accrediting and oversight bodies. With deference to President Eisenhower, who coined the term *military industrial complex*, I refer to this panoply of interests as the *medical administrative complex*, or *MAC* for short.

As we'll explore in this book, MAC is a busy guy. Always with an agenda of "doing what's best for us," he creates problems. And then makes a comfortable living going through the motions of fixing them. He likes to micro-manage things with arcane rules. But his natural tendency is to resist the kinds of major structural changes that could threaten his influence or livelihood in any way. MAC likes his job.

The Economic Human and the Next Curve

Rational choice theory is the economic principle that says informed people are inclined to make those decisions, among available options, that give them the greatest value and satisfaction. Economists refer to this behavioral characteristic as *homo economicus,* otherwise known as the economic human.

One of the major—and historically legitimate—arguments that academics and others have expressed about the medical marketplace concerns the lack of objective, quantitative measures of value in health care. This, it is said, has resulted in a market that simply doesn't have the clear-cut signals that it needs to inform rational product, pricing, and consumption decisions.

But this is no longer the case. With the exploding universe of Big Data and all of its enabling information products, all parties to the health care transaction—consumers, purchasers, and caregivers—are increasingly able to access the rich information they need to make informed, rational decisions. Health care services and their costs and outcomes can now be measured, tracked, and compared. Consumers are demanding new products and approaches to health services delivery. The market is defining value.

This is the essence of the Next Curve: *Market-driven, with affordable access and consumer options. Product innovation and diversity. Informed consumers making rational choices on the basis of comparative value. A competitive market discipline. Powerful incentives for continuous product improvement* (Figure 1.2).

In the Next Curve it is an empowered market—the economic human—that is defining and measuring value, and that is the driving force of innovation and change. Our pal MAC becomes less and less relevant in this new future of health care.

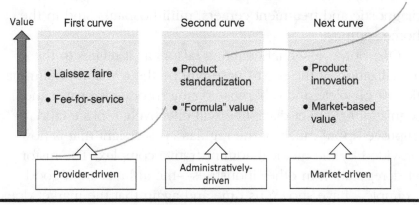

Figure 1.2 Value in the Next Curve.

Fast Forward: A New Future

In this book we'll describe how the health care industry in the new future of the Next Curve differs from the current state.

One of the most fundamental shifts in the Next Curve will be to change the manner in which health care is financed. Insurance will be restored to its original purpose and functionality. Consumers will have genuine product choices when it comes to benefit features, deductibles, and so on. The key to making this happen will be the development of expanded, sustainable safety nets, and to clearly distinguish the role of the safety nets from the private insurance market. The industry will move away from its current production-oriented, fee-for-service reimbursement approach, and complete the transition toward true value-based, market-driven payment methodologies.

As financing and payment models evolve, market forces will complete the evolution of health care delivery from the existing provider-centric model to one that is truly centered on the patient and the patient's disease and conditions. Services will be structured and coordinated in a way that wrap around the full scope of services through the continuum of prevention, diagnosis, treatment, and recovery. For most patients, services will be provided in accessible high-tech diagnostic and treatment centers, mini-hospitals, and in the home setting.

One of the essential enabling factors as it relates to the actualization of the Next Curve will be the revision or elimination of obsolete and otherwise counterproductive rules and regulations. Market discipline will effectively replace (and improve upon) much of the regulatory oversight that is now provided by the medical-administrative complex. The history of deregulation in other industries—the airlines are a good example—have shown us time and again that the market does a far better job.

This Book: A Look Ahead

This book is structured to answer the following basic questions:

- How and why is the U.S. health care industry so basically dysfunctional?
- What are the forces at work that are pushing both stasis and change?
- Where is the industry headed in the Next Curve?
- What are the TRANSFORMATIONAL GOALS that lead us toward actualization of the Next Curve?
- For each Transformational Goal, what are the major things—THE ESSENTIAL STEPS—that must be accomplished?

In SECTION I: INDUSTRY DYSFUNCTION: ITS ROOT CAUSES AND EFFECTS, we'll proceed in the next chapter to examine the major challenges facing the health care industry (Chapter 2: "Health Care's Perfect Storm"). As part of this narrative, we'll look at a momentum scenario: where health care in the U.S. is inevitably headed if we're not able to make fundamental changes to the existing industry model.

In the succeeding Section I chapters we'll examine the root causes of industry dysfunction in more detail: the drawbacks of existing safety net and insurance models in Chapter 3 ("What Happened to Health Insurance?"); the problems with existing reimbursement methodologies in Chapter 4 ("Follow the Money: A Broken Payment Model"); the fragmentation of health services delivery in Chapter 5 ("Silos, Everywhere"); and the problems that stem from our existing regulatory structure as discussed in Chapter 6 ("The Real Costs of Regulation"). In Chapter 7 ("Where's the Competition?"), we'll examine the existing industry structure and how conflicting policy directions have eroded competition.

As additional background perspective on the seminal causes of current industry dysfunction, I urge readers to refer to the Appendix: "How We Got Here—A Brief History of Health Care in the U.S." This is a look at the chronology of political and regulatory milestones going all the way back to the early part of the twentieth century. It reminds us of why Einstein was so spot-on in his observations about insanity.

Next, we'll look at the scenario of a universal, single payer model, and how this would affect the availability and quality of health care in the U.S. (Chapter 8: "Why Government Health Care Isn't the Answer"). As the chapter title suggests, this isn't an argument for government-run health care. In fact, its thrust is to give us a perspective on what *not* to do. In this chapter we'll start to frame the argument for a more market-driven, consumer-oriented future state that is the Next Curve of health care.

We'll conclude Section I with Chapter 9 ("Market Disruptors and Transformers") by looking at the technological and market dynamics that are driving industry change. These include the enabling influences of Big Data and precision medicine, as well as disruptive delivery platforms and industry fusion phenomena that are changing the market landscape.

In SECTION II: HEALTH CARE IN THE NEXT CURVE: A ROADMAP TO INDUSTRY TRANSFORMATION, we'll begin Chapter 10 ("Destinations of the Next Curve") by describing the Next Curve in terms of the principal destinations of *access*, *choice*, and *value*. We'll then proceed to identify the Transformational Goals that are critical to attaining the Next Curve.

The chapters that follow in Section II spell out 30 Essential Steps—the things that must be done to achieve the Transformational Goals. For starters, we need to ensure that we have the right safety nets in place (Chapter 11: "First, the Safety Nets"). This provides the flexibility to restructure existing insurance models, as will be described in Chapter 12 ("Insurance and Choice, Once Again"), and to make the needed changes in how we pay providers (Chapter 13: "From Production to Value").

The redesign of insurance and payer models provides the market ecosystem necessary to change how health care services are structured and delivered; and specifically, the transition to a system that is designed around the needs of patients and their conditions. This is a central element of the Next Curve, and is described in Chapter 14 ("No More Silos: Patient-Centered Care in the Next Curve").

In order to complete the journey of transformation, it will be essential to eliminate or substantially revise the regulations that are currently blocking progressive change. These are spelled out in Chapter 15 ("Less Regulation, Better Health Care").

Finally, in Chapter 16 ("Positioning Strategies for the New Future"), we'll look at the real-world impacts of the Next Curve on the industry, and how traditional health care organizations need to reposition their product and platform strategies to be successful in a market-driven health care world. We'll discuss how industry transformation in the Next Curve can give renewed purpose, focus, and energy to caregivers and institutions.

References

1. I. Morrison, *The Second Curve*, Ballentine Books, New York, 1997.
2. M. E. Porter, What is value in health care? *New England Journal of Medicine*, 363(26): 2477–2481, 2010.
3. American Hospital Association, Committee on Research, *Your Hospital's Path to the Second Curve: Integration and Transformation*, Health Research & Educational Trust, Chicago, IL, 2014.
4. C. Beasley, The triple aim: Optimizing health, care, and cost, *Healthcare Executive*, 24: 64–65, 2009.

Chapter 2

Health Care's Perfect Storm

"The first step toward change is awareness. The second step is acceptance."

—Nathaniel Braden, Psychotherapist

CHAPTER OVERVIEW

- The U.S. has the most advanced medicine among top industrial countries, but the highest costs and the worst health indicators.
- With the combined effects of demographic and disease trends, we face a scenario of spiraling resource consumption and rising costs.
- We're approaching the upper limit of what society is willing (or realistically able) to spend on health care.
- We face a scenario of stringent rationing if we don't make fundamental changes to the existing industry model.

The Gathering Forces

Several years ago my consulting team was asked to work with the County of San Bernardino, California. Our task was to assess health conditions in the county, and to help reposition the county-owned health care system to better meet the needs of local residents.

It was a mind-opening exercise. When we did our analysis of the county's demographic and morbidity profiles, things didn't add up. The level of chronic disease was off the charts, particularly as we looked at the prevalence of heart disease, stroke, diabetes, cancer, and depression. Just by looking at the morbidity data alone, you could easily conclude that we were looking at a very old population. But we weren't. The average age of the San Bernardino population was, and still is, much below the national average. So what accounted for this apparent anomaly?

This phenomenon was not due to poor health care services. The area is primarily served by the San Bernardino County health system and by Loma Linda University Health— both former client organizations and arguably among some of the finest health institutions in the country. Nor was access an issue. Covered by a large and progressive Medi-Cal health plan, an unusually high percentage of low-income residents had access to health care. Ironically, one of the healthiest communities on the planet—a so-called Blue Zone—is located right next door in Loma Linda, California. No, what we determined was that the causes of this unusual prevalence of chronic disease boiled down to a combination of socio-economic factors and unhealthy lifestyle behaviors. These factors have resulted in a pattern of chronic diseases that is usually associated with a much older population.

Sadly, the disease profile that we observed in San Bernardino isn't an isolated case. It's increasingly the pattern—especially in lower-income communities—throughout the United States. My team found a similar pattern in certain community areas in Chicago while doing work with the Cook County Health and Hospitals System.

There are a lot of co-determinants to be sure, but income and lifestyle factors account for much of this pattern. The prevalence of obesity—particularly childhood and adolescent obesity—fueled by unhealthy diets and limited physical activity, is giving rise to a chain of chronic disease: diabetes, heart disease, stroke, arthritis, premature joint deterioration, and a host of secondary diseases, including cancer. These morbidity factors compound as a given population grows older.

It is estimated that by 2025, chronic diseases will affect nearly 165 million persons in the U.S.[1] As shown in Figure 2.1, stroke, cardiovascular disease, diabetes, and hypertension lead the pack in terms of projected prevalence.

Chronic diseases consume most of our health care resources. They account for over 75% of total dollars spent on health care. They're responsible for the vast majority of physician office visits and about 80% of hospital admissions. They are literally the lifeblood of the pharmaceutical industry, with over 90% of prescriptions relating to some form of chronic disease. Overall, the health care costs for individuals with at least one chronic condition is typically about five times higher than for those without such a condition.

As we look forward, the outlook is less than encouraging. Yes, we can expect that advances in medical science,

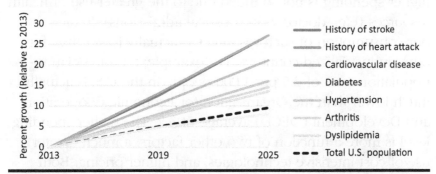

Figure 2.1   Projected growth in population with chronic conditions (2013–2025). (From Health Affairs, 2013.)

including the huge strides being made in genomic research, will have a positive impact on both the prevalence and treatment of chronic disease. But such progress will likely be more than offset by the double whammy of an aging population—the *silver tsunami*—and the growing prevalence of chronic disease within younger population segments. It's health care's perfect storm.

What's Wrong with This Picture?

The United States has world-leading medical schools, stellar research, and the most advanced technologies. We have first-rate health care systems and highly competent caregivers. If a family member or I have health issues and need the best medical care possible, there's no other place I would rather be.

So why, with such incredible medical talent and a wealth of resources at our disposal, is our health care industry so fundamentally dysfunctional? It's hugely expensive. Health outcomes don't compare favorably with those of other countries. It's not patient-friendly and is often difficult to navigate. There's an inconsistency of both quality and costs across different health systems and locales.

At nearly 18% of GDP, our health care costs are by far the highest among the top industrialized nations (Figure 2.2). The higher spending is not so much due to the greater use of health resources (e.g., doctor visits, hospital admissions). In fact, our consumption of such resources is actually lower than for other industrialized countries. For example, the physician-to-population ratio of 2.5 per 1,000 people in the U.S. is actually much lower than the Organization for Economic Cooperation and Development (OECD) average of 3.2. The higher spending level is more a function of two other factors: a much greater use of cost-intensive technologies, and higher pricing. Both of these factors are driven by an industry structure and payer methodology that incentivizes resource consumption. At the

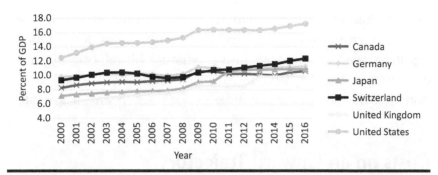

Figure 2.2 Health care costs of select OECD countries (2000–2016). (From Health Statistics, Organization for Economic Cooperation and Development (OECD), Paris, France, 2017.)

same time, we spend far less than many other countries on social services and overall prevention.

But despite all the resources that we expend on health care, *our outcomes rank at or near the bottom.* Based on a key indicator—life expectancy at birth—the U.S. ranks 34th among the top industrial countries (Figure 2.3).

The directional trend is not encouraging. The average life expectancy at birth declined in 2016 for the first time in 22 years, going to 78.8 years from 78.9 years. Much of this decline is attributed to the sharp spike in substance abuse and opioid-related deaths.

The less-than-stellar outcome measures of health care in the U.S. are not due so much to poor health care as they are due to *poor health.* Americans are less healthy and die younger

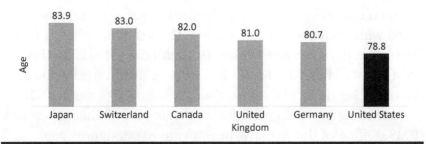

Figure 2.3 Life expectancy at birth of select OECD countries (2015). (From OECD, Paris, France, 2015.)

than people in other rich nations. This is largely due to the lifestyle factors cited earlier and related behaviors, for example, smoking, teen pregnancies and premature births, obesity, and drug usage. And the people who face high risk factors often don't get the health care they need. Or they receive it too late.

Costs on an Upward Trajectory

When the Affordable Care Act was passed in 2010, its supporters projected that it would translate into substantial cost reductions across the board. President Obama publically predicted that the typical family would see a yearly $2,500 reduction in their health care costs. Obamacare supporters have pointed to the overall moderation in the rate of health care spending increases that has prevailed in recent years as proof that the plan did in fact reduce costs as intended.

But this moderation in spending growth was already underway when the ACA was passed due to the impact of the economic recession, and continued in large part because of the slowness of the economy to rebound. When you factor in what economists call *excess inflation*, which is the rate of inflation that exceeds the overall growth in gross domestic product, the slowdown has been far less pronounced. Still, any way you parse the numbers, the costs are staggering. The average per-person health care costs now exceed $10,000 a year.

This is a major and growing burden on the typical family that has seen continued increases in health insurance premiums, combined with skyrocketing deductibles. The real pain index is what people are paying out-of-pocket for health care. Based on the latest statistics from the Kaiser Foundation, the average worker's out-of-pocket deductibles have risen by nearly 50% since 2011.[2]

According to the Centers for Medicare and Medicaid Services (CMS) Office of the Actuary, health care expenditures are projected to grow at an average annual rate of 5.8% over at least the next decade. The per capita health insurance bill

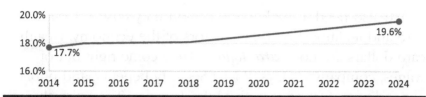

Figure 2.4 National health care spending as a percent of GDP (2014–2024). (From Congressional Budget Office, Washington, DC.)

is expected to rise from the current level of over $7,500 per year (2017) to nearly $12,000 in 2024, a 60% increase. The Congressional Budget Office (CBO) is projecting that job-based premiums will rise by about the same rate over this timeline.

These increases in spending levels will bump up the health care share of the economy from the current level of 18% of GDP to closer to 20% within the next five years (Figure 2.4).

Heading toward a Spending Ceiling

Will we really be spending 20% or more of our national product on health care? Are we on a trajectory of virtually unlimited spending? Many industry analysts, including this author, believe that we're approaching the outer limits of what we're willing or realistically able to spend on health care.

It's important to note that the projections coming out of CMS and CBO are based on past trends and certain empirical assumptions about the future. But as we're witnessing in other sectors of our society and economy, those assumptions don't always hold up. They don't take into account prevailing social and political trends. In other words, they don't factor in human behavior.

Among other things, we need to understand that health care is not necessarily the highest priority for the U.S. public. It's interesting to note that in the last national election, health care was not even close to the top of the list of concerns or priorities expressed by the public in the various polls.

We also need to look at the opportunity cost of health care and its impact on other sectors of the economy. Health care dollars are not *extra dollars*. They come right out of wages, company outlays, Social Security benefits, and public expenditures for services and infrastructure. They directly impact what consumers are able to spend on other goods and services. While average middle-income household expenditures for most basic essentials have actually declined in the post-recession period, health care outlays continue to go up. Health care is one of the major reasons for personal bankruptcies.

There are other reasons why we can't just look at past trends to predict the future. One is the overall trend in medicine toward more prevention and treatment in less cost-intensive modalities, including outpatient and home care. In addition, insurance companies and employers are reaching a point where they're less inclined to increase their outlays year after year, and are now passing more of these increases off to the consumers of health care. Consumers are balking at these increases as well.

A colleague, Jeff Bauer, and his coauthor Mark Hagland state the case of why we may be reaching the outer limits of health care spending in their book: *Paradox and Imperatives in Health Care*.[3] These analysts—along with this author—don't believe that we can extrapolate past trends in health care spending to predict future patterns, and point out the danger in applying standard prediction methodology to an industry that is going through profound change.

Is Rationing the Default Scenario?

So what happens when the upward slope of the cost curve hits the ceiling of what we're willing to spend? We have people telling us who gets what kinds of services and how much of each. It's called rationing.

This is not an unrealistic scenario. In fact, the enabling policy infrastructure for rationing was put in place under Obamacare with provisions for the Independent Payment Advisory Board (IPAB). Modeled after a similar authority structure used by the British health system, IPAB has been described by many as our very own version of UK's *death panel*. We'll be looking at the potential implications IPAB or IPAB-like agencies in more detail in Chapter 8 ("Why Government Health Care Isn't the Answer").

Pending efforts to repeal or substantially modify Obamacare may end the likes of IPAB. But unless we can do something to address the core problems of our existing health care model, we'll inevitably be facing a future of stringent rationing and government micro-management.

One thing we do know. The existing health industry model is not sustainable, at least not in its current state.

References

1. T. M. Dahl et al., *An Aging Population and Growing Disease Burden Will Require a Large and Specialized Health Care Workforce By 2025*, Health Affairs, November, 2013.
2. Kaiser/HRET Survey of Employer-Sponsored Benefits, 2011–2016.
3. J. C. Bauer and M. Hagland, *Paradox and Imperatives in Health Care: How Efficiency, Effectiveness, and E-Transformation Can Conquer Waste and Optimize Quality*, CRC Press, Boca Raton, FL, 2007.

Chapter 3

What Happened to Health Insurance?

"America doesn't have health insurance."

—Joe Biden

CHAPTER OVERVIEW

■ Many in the U.S. still don't have affordable access to care.
■ The individual insurance market has become restrictive and expensive.
■ Insurance regulations distort the market, resulting in higher prices.
■ The traditional employer health plan carries with it hidden costs and inequities.
■ Neither Medicare nor Medicaid are sustainable in their current form.

A Perfectly Dysfunctional Model

Greg, a friend of mine, called recently to discuss his health insurance dilemma. Several years ago he left a well-paying job as a senior executive at a large bank and started his own financial advisory services firm. The business has done well. Greg and his wife Kris are in good health, and at the age of 54 aren't in the phase of life where they'll be growing their family. "So how is it," Greg asked, "that our insurance premium is going up close to 25% this year? That will be like a 55% increase in just three years!" He went on to complain about his options, or lack thereof. "Hey, we don't need maternity coverage," he pointed out. "We exercise regularly. And neither of us consumes alcohol or uses drugs. We neither need nor want to pay a premium that is priced to cover these things. We're just not sure of what to do or where to go for our insurance."

They're not alone. The individual market has traditionally been an available—and mostly affordable option—for the self-employed, early retirees, and other workers who aren't covered under employer plans or under Medicare or Medicaid. Under the Affordable Care Act (ACA), this market has become much more regulated, and costs have skyrocketed. The essential benefits provisions and community-rating requirements haven't helped. And to be sure, Greg and Kris have done a lot better than most. Based on a recent report, per-member-per-month (PMPM) costs in the individual market rose by over 75% in the three-year period that Greg was referring to.[1]

Let's say that you're shopping for home insurance. You want to protect against major catastrophes, for example, fire or a tornado. You know that, over time, your home will need repainting or the furnace repaired. You also know that on a regular basis you'll need to have the lawn mown, and that you'll be paying for a housekeeper to do routine cleaning.

So do you buy an insurance policy that covers all of these expenses? Or do you want to just protect yourself against major disasters, and pay for the rest out of your own pocket? Or maybe you want to supplement your homeowners' insurance with a warranty plan that covers appliance repairs. And you can, if you wish, earmark some savings in your bank account to be used for unexpected repairs.

The answers to these questions will, of course, vary according to an individual's financial status, needs, tolerance for risk, and so on. In any case, the person who purchases insurance to cover routine or predictable expenses knows, or at least should know, that it's no more than a form of prepayment.

We used to think of health insurance in much the same way. It was essentially the shared pooling of resources to compensate individuals who suffer unexpected illness or injury. The individual's premium contribution to the pool would typically reflect some actuarial predictability—based on factors such as age and gender—regarding the likelihood of incurring expenses. But, as Greg and Kris have discovered, we have distorted this basic concept to the point where so much of what passes for health insurance isn't really insurance anymore.

Overall, the way we go about financing our health care in the U.S. is a perfect model of dysfunction. Practically speaking, it doesn't really meet any of our needs. With the passage of the ACA, we have somehow managed to find a way of improving access for the few at the expense of the many. Despite federal and state initiatives spanning multiple generations, we still have quite a significant number of people who still lack affordable access to health care. Mandated benefits dictate expensive products that many don't want or need. And the playing field is anything but level, as individuals in employer-sponsored plans continue to have tax advantages that the rest of the market doesn't enjoy. Finally, we have safety nets in the form of Medicare and Medicaid that aren't sustainable, at least not in their current form.

Affordable Access: Still No Fix

The 2010 Affordable Care Act has in many respects been the biggest change to U.S. health care since the passage of Medicare-Medicaid. The Act was intended to expand health plan coverage to the uninsured and reduce health care costs. This was done through the introduction of insurance mandates, subsidies, and exchanges. The law in effect required health plans to accept all applicants, cover a specified range of conditions, and be priced at certain levels regardless of any pre-existing conditions. The ACA also extended coverage for young persons under the age of 26 as part of their family plan.

Sounds good, right? Why then, has the Obamacare ship hit such rough waters?

The ACA has failed primarily because the insurance products that have evolved are out of sync with the market. Obamacare has boxed insurers into providing highly expensive policies with more coverage than many individuals need, want, or can afford. Despite the mandates, many people, particularly younger folks, aren't buying the product. The penalties for not getting coverage are relatively low compared with high premiums and the unlikely probability of getting sick. And then there are people in situations such as Greg and Kris who find it difficult if not impossible to find products that meet their specific needs.

To make matters worse, people have the option of signing up *after* they became ill and need financial assistance. The plans can't exclude people with pre-existing conditions. All of this has had the combined effect of reducing the total premium dollars, while skewing the risk pool toward a less healthy population. This is not a sound actuarial equation, any way you slice it.

Despite the intentions of the ACA, we still have a sizeable population group in the insured category. Figure 3.1 shows the distribution of the U.S. population today, by type of coverage.

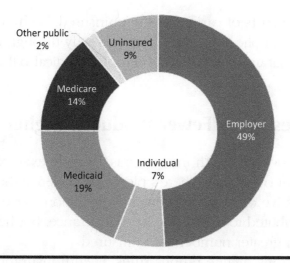

Figure 3.1   Health insurance in the U.S. (From The Henry J. Kaiser Family Foundation, Menlo Park, CA.)

Employer-sponsored health plans are by far the single largest source of coverage, accounting for nearly half of the U.S. population. This is followed in order by Medicaid, Medicare, and non-group coverage. The expanded coverage brought about by the Affordable Care Act notwithstanding, we still have over 28 million people, or about 9% of the population, who don't have health insurance.

There are multiple reasons why so many remain uninsured. Predictably, cost is the major reason. Many individuals are in low-income families that have at least one family member in the work force, but not in employment situations that give them group coverage. Even for those individuals who can access coverage through their employers, the premiums can be out of reach from an affordability standpoint. A number of uninsured adults are in what's referred to as the *coverage gap*. They earn too much to qualify for Medicaid, but not enough to meet the threshold for tax credits under the provisions of the Health Insurance Exchanges.

The plight of the uninsured remains a problem of major concern. From a care delivery standpoint, it can restrict or delay access for many. And in economic terms, we as a society assume the costs of caring for the uninsured, both directly in the form of public assistance, and indirectly through invisible subsidies that are baked into everyone's medical bills.

Mandates Mean Fewer Products, Higher Prices

The regulation of health insurance is a classic example of government overreach. There's plenty of evidence that shows how excessive or counterproductive regulations have not only contributed to the high cost of insurance, but have also resulted in greater numbers of uninsured.

Regulations dictate ratings rules. Health insurance companies subsist by pooling and redistributing risk, with premiums that are based on the risk profile of the individual policy holder. When the government restricts insurance companies from applying certain criteria to underwriting decisions, the only recourse is to charge higher premiums for all.

For example, rating rules that enable high-risk enrollees to obtain insurance at a low cost will invariably raise the costs of premiums for healthier enrollees. When younger and healthier persons can't afford the premiums or decide that they don't want to pay the price, this further skews the risk pool in a way that makes insurance more expensive for everyone. It's called adverse selection. The net result is that the insurance rules make insurance prohibitively costly for many people. In certain states it's impossible to buy a plan that only provides catastrophic coverage.

State insurance regulations also specify so-called mandated benefits. Service mandates dictate the coverage requirements for specific medical conditions. Provider mandates require that insurers offer coverage for various types of providers, such as chiropractors or podiatrists.

Several years ago some landmark research conducted by The Heritage Foundation looked at the correlation of the number of mandates at the state level with the cost of insurance on a state-by-state basis. The results, predictably, showed that insurance premiums were statistically higher in the states that regulate most heavily.[2]

Employer Health Plans: Not What They're Cracked Up to Be

Many years ago there were mining towns where workers could only buy their goods at a company store. The company store might offer a "discount" and convince the employees that this was a benefit above and beyond their usual wages. But in reality, the employees were paying for the full cost plus overhead in lieu of wages. And because they didn't really have a basis of comparison with what the product might cost in a competitive market, they often wound up paying a lot more than they would otherwise. The company store was only too happy to have the workers fill up their carts, and wasn't too concerned about the wholesale prices since it would all be passed on to the workers in any case. And the company could consider any *unreimbursed* costs as tax-deductible expenses.

Today we have a modern-day equivalent of the company store. It's called the employer health care plan.

As referenced above, employer-sponsored health plans now account for the largest single group of beneficiaries (Figure 3.1). It's a very popular model and is easily the most prized benefit in any employment situation. But the employer health plan is not all what it's cracked up to be. It poses a hidden cost burden on employees, and limits their flexibility in a number of ways. And it creates an unfair tax advantage for both employers and their employees.

The way employee health insurance is treated from a tax standpoint is mostly a holdover from WWII when employers used *free* health insurance as a way of making up the restrictions on wage increases. The tax exemption was formally codified into law in 1954, and has since been a way for employees to receive non-taxable income in the form of health insurance. Until the passage of the ACA, there was basically no limit to the value of health benefits that can go untaxed.

The tax provision for employer health insurance has a number of problems, and has probably affected the delivery and cost of health care more than any other single factor. The rich benefits paid for by third parties effectively hide the cost of care, which leads to more consumption. It creates an uneven playing field, since only those who work for employers with group health plans are able to take advantage of the tax benefit. This is patently unfair to the growing number of workers who are self-employed, part-time, or who work for smaller companies who do not provide employee health benefits.

Although employers brag about their rich health benefits, they actually favor the employer over the employee. Employers are able to pay employees a significant portion of their total compensation in the form of benefits versus cash, benefitting from the tax exemption. The employee only sees the portion of the health premium that they are contributing, often not realizing that they are in effect contributing the unseen portion as well.

Employer-sponsored health insurance carries a high price tag for the country overall. The exemption is one of the largest loopholes in the federal tax code, costing the federal treasury on the order of $250 billion per year.[3] This is actually a stealth tax on all of us, whether we derive any benefit or not. It creates a significant disparity in the marketplace. For the growing number of workers who don't have access to group insurance, there's no tax subsidy. And without this tax subsidy, people face inherently higher prices and fewer options for coverage.

Because employers can effectively use tax-free benefits as a means of competing for employees, the evolution of the plans has been toward high-end pricing and super-low deductibles. The deductibles have in many instances become so low that they cover just about everything, including totally routine medical expenses that could not in any way be considered unpredictable, insurable events within the traditional definition of insurance. This has made consumers much less price-sensitive when it comes to medical services, and at the same time has contributed significantly to an evolving mind-set that health care should somehow be something that "we shouldn't have to pay for."

The fact that employees don't have a lot of concern about health care prices has led insurance companies to basically negotiate the prices with providers on the side, and without a lot of consumer awareness or concern. Providers can raise prices as well and pass these increases off to the insurance companies, who are then able to raise their premiums to make up for the difference. In the end, the employee/consumer is picking up the total tab, but is usually oblivious to this.

Another problem with the employer group model (yes, there are so many problems) is that it imposes restrictions on an individual's ability to transfer health insurance from one employer to another. The reason for this links directly to the tax laws referenced earlier. In order to be eligible for the pre-tax deductibility provisions, the plan has to fall in the category of group insurance. So, by definition, the employee loses this insurance when they change jobs. This can result in *job lock* situations where individuals feel that they can't leave their jobs. In fact, most states strictly prohibit employers from buying any form of individual insurance that could be taken from job to job with pre-tax dollars.

The central issue at stake is not with employer-provided insurance, per se. This is, and should remain, between the employer and the employee. *But we shouldn't penalize people who don't have this benefit available to them.* We shouldn't force individuals to buy health insurance, and then kick them in the pants by telling them they're going to be paying one-third more because they've got to pay with after-tax dollars.

Needless to say, any changes to the employer health model won't come easy. The country as a whole has become highly inured to the whole idea of employer-sponsored health plans. But we need to understand both the economic and practical consequences of such plans, and how they may not be in the best interest of either the covered employees or the public in general. We also need to understand what options to revising this prevailing model might be considered.

Medicare Trouble Ahead

Medicare for all has become an oft-heard mantra for certain politicians and others who support a single payer, universal health model. Without question Medicare has been a highly popular program. But it's not without its problems. In fact, the current model is not sustainable without major changes to its overall structure and benefits design.

Signed into law in 1965, Medicare functions as a single payer social insurance program that now provides insurance coverage for over 55 million seniors and others with disabilities. The program is funded through a combination of payroll tax, premiums from beneficiaries, and general tax revenues. Medicare Part A covers hospital and hospice services, while Part B pays for outpatient services, and Part D, prescription drugs. Generally speaking, Medicare covers about one-half of the various charges for enrollees. Many cover at least a portion of their remaining costs with a supplemental insurance policy through Medicare Advantage.

The demographic trends are working against Medicare. We have the confluence of two phenomena: an aging population, combined with a work force that's shrinking relative to the size of the retiree group. Fifty years ago, when Medicare was enacted, the average life expectancy was 70.2 years. It's now closer to 80 years. And while there are currently about three working individuals per Medicare recipient, this ratio will decline to less than 2.5 by 2030. Since it's the working population that funds the program, that's a problem. Retirees often have the mistaken notion that they have paid for the benefits they receive. But the reality is that Medicare benefits for enrollees exceed their contributions by a factor of about three-to-one.[4]

So, no wonder people like the "Medicare for all" proposition. But as you can readily see, "Medicare for some" for some has a decidedly different economic structure than "Medicare for all."

Medicare is already trillions of dollars in long-term *debt*. The size of that debt is projected to grow significantly in the years ahead. The current Medicare spending level of $717 billion is expected to exceed $1.2 trillion by 2024, approaching 4.5% of GDP (Figure 3.2).[5]

In addition to the demographic problem, Medicare has serious structural issues. Medicare suffers from an outdated, defined benefits model design, and a bureaucratic rigidity that makes it seemingly incapable of modernizing and competing in a more market-driven environment. There are significant gaps in coverage. Compliance requirements restrict treatment options for patients and caregivers. This is not to mention the huge levels of waste, as well as fraud and abuse that are estimated to be about 30% of total outlays.[6]

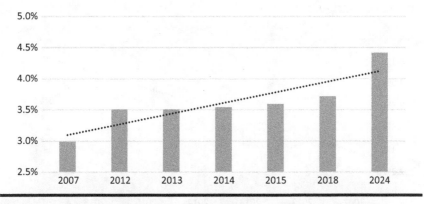

Figure 3.2 Projected Medicare spending as a percent of GDP (2007–2024). (From Health Affairs, 2015.)

Medicaid Also Facing an Uncertain Future

Medicaid is another politically popular program that is facing some major demographic, structural, and fiscal challenges. Originally set up as a sibling program to Medicare, Medicaid was intended to be a jointly funded federal and state welfare program for low-income women and children. The scope of Medicaid has expanded significantly over the years to include other beneficiaries, including millions who have been made eligible for Medicaid under Obamacare. At the same time, the extent of covered services has increased significantly. Today, Medicaid is the second-largest category of health care beneficiaries, covering close to 20% of the population (Figure 3.1).

Along with the expansion of Medicaid, we've seen sharp rises in spending at both federal and state levels. Based on the current trajectory, it's estimated that the total spending level will balloon from approximately $530 billion in 2015 to $835 billion by 2024, approaching 3.3% of GDP (Figure 3.3).[7]

These projections are based on the current program structure established under the provisions of the ACA. As of this writing, this is still the operative program. Sadly, as is the case with Medicare, Medicaid has been a breeding ground for fraud and abuse, amounting to significant dollars and drains on federal and state budgets.

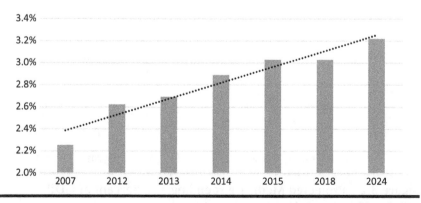

Figure 3.3   Projected Medicaid spending as a percent of GDP (2007–2024). (From Health Affairs, 2015.)

Another major impact on Medicaid is the tremendous growth of the elderly segment as the baby-boomers enter the retirement years. Most have not saved adequately to pay for the long-term care costs that are not picked up by Medicare, and will wind up on Medicaid as a means of paying for nursing home care and other long-term care expenses. This is a fiscal time bomb that is silently ticking away. Currently this age group is a little over one-third of Medicaid enrollment, but already accounts for a disproportionate share of total program spending.

Getting access to providers is another problem for Medicaid recipients. The expansion under the ACA succeeded in bringing many new enrollees into the program. But this doesn't guarantee that individuals will be able to see a given caregiver. Typically Medicaid reimburses providers at a level that is about two-thirds of what Medicare pays. This factor, combined with the burdensome and time-consuming reimbursement processes that providers encounter, limits the number of doctors and other caregivers who are willing to accept Medicaid patients. Based on research conducted by the Centers for Disease Control and Prevention, over 30% of providers are not willing to accept Medicaid patients.[8]

One Size Doesn't Fit All

So, getting back to Greg and Kris's situation described earlier, what was their solution? They got out of the traditional insurance market altogether and, instead, joined a health care savings plan sponsored by a religious association, where the members pay a certain dollar amount to their own savings account. Participating members commit to a healthy life style, including abstention from drugs and alcohol. When they or another member incurs expenses, approved amounts are paid directly to providers who are part of a PPO. For people like Greg and Kris—healthy individuals who eschew alcohol and drugs—this option can make a lot of sense.

Going forward, we need to provide the needed safety nets for segments of the population that don't have adequate health care coverage. *But we don't need to turn the market upside down for everyone else.* We don't need to totally disrupt the health care coverage of 91% of the population in the quest to take care of the other 9%. One size does not fit all.

In Section II, we'll look at some very specific things that can be done to ensure affordable access for disenfranchised population segments. This can be done while giving the overall consumer population more choices, and at the same time, remedying some of the inequities in the current model.

References

1. *An Analysis of Individual and Small Group Health Insurance Trends*, Healthcare Business Advisor, Mark Farrah Associates, June 5, 2017.
2. M. J. New, *The Effect of State Regulations on Health Insurance Premiums: A Preliminary Analysis*, The Heritage Foundation, October 27, 2005, Washington, DC.
3. J. Antos, *End the Tax Exemption for Employer-Provided Health Care, The New York Times*, December 6, 2016.
4. C. Conover, *Sorry Seniors, You Didn't Pay for (All of) That*, Urban Institute study, *Forbes*, December 3, 2012, New York.
5. Management Challenge 2: Fighting Fraud, Waste, and Abuse in Medicare Parts A and B, Congressional Budget Office, Updated Budget Projections: 2014 to 2024, April 2014.
6. Office of Inspector General, HHS, 2015.
7. CMS, Actuarial Report on the Financial Outlook for Medicaid, 2014.
8. E. Hing, S. L. Decker, and E. Jamoom, *Acceptance of New Patients with Public and Private Insurance by Office-Based Physicians: United States, 2013*, Centers for Disease Control and Prevention, National Center for Health Statistics Data Brief No. 195, March 2015, Hyattsville, MD.

Chapter 4

Follow the Money:
A Broken Payment Model

"In this world you get what you pay for."

—Kurt Vonnegut, Jr., The Cat's Cradle

CHAPTER OVERVIEW

- The third-party payer model insulates both providers and consumers from the economic consequences of their decisions.
- Fee-for-service leads to more utilization, overpricing, and waste.
- Both providers and payers are buried in deep layers of administrative and overhead costs.
- The move toward value-based payment methodologies is a positive direction, however...
- We need to look at new ways of measuring and comparing value.

Why Not "Food Insurance?"

Mark J. Perry, author and economics professor at the University of Michigan, shared an interesting perspective on the way we pay for health care services: "Imagine if grocery shopping worked like health insurance," he offered. "Let's call it 'food insurance.' Now let's imagine what actually shopping for groceries would look like. Your food insurance qualifies you to a specified number of visits to your local food provider. If you visit in-network food providers you pay only a small co-pay, but if you visit out-of-network food providers, you pay a higher co-pay. (If you have emergency munchies and need fast food, you pay an even higher co-pay to get prepared meals handed to you at a drive thru.)"

"The important thing," he went on, "is that you don't actually pay for your food on a per-item basis. In fact, you don't even know what it costs. When you walk into your primary food care provider, all of the items are there on the shelves, but there are no prices. That's because the cost of your shopping trip is already covered by your food care insurance. It's the whole reason that you have it. So you would get your shopping cart and go down the aisles, putting as much food as you felt you needed into your cart." He continued, "To make this example realistic, however, let's assume that you can't resell any of the food. Do you think people would get more or less food in the food insurance scenario versus in the real world, where we pay for everything item-by-item? They'd probably get much more in the food insurance scenario. This idea is called *overutilization*, and it might be one reason that American health care costs arc so high."[1]

Dr. Perry's analogy isn't at all far-fetched. In fact, he may have understated the problem in one sense. In the case of health care, the grocer (provider) is only too anxious to pile more items into your cart. And to make matters worse, the folks who are picking up the tab (third-party payers) can always just raise their prices to make up for any increases in wholesale costs, or for that matter, any inefficiencies or waste. As a result, *we have a combination of over-ordering, over-pricing, and wasteful consumption.* It explains how a hospital can charge $25 for an aspirin pill. And why a given procedure in the same community can cost three or four times as much at one hospital versus another. And it explains a lot about why the U.S. has a health care spending level that is by far the highest among industrialized nations.

With third-party payer economics, both patient and provider are removed from the economic consequences of care decisions. The bills are paid by someone else. Most health care is, of course, financed through the government and by employers. Third-party payers are responsible for much of the decision-making as it relates to coverage provisions and pricing. The result is that virtually all parties to the health care transaction are a step removed from the consequences of their decisions. The insurance intermediator and the government create walls of separation between the producers and consumers of services. This gets in the way of the usual market signals that drive demand, supply, and pricing decisions. It's a unique, and inherently artificial, construct.

The implications of this dynamic can be seen in the relationship between *actuarial value* (the portion of expenses the health plan will pay versus the deductible) and the utilization of health services. Based on research conducted by the RAND Corporation, the level of aggregate expenditures for individuals who have a 30% deductible plan is nearly one-fourth less than for those who have no deductible outlays.[2]

This isn't to say that low deductible or prepaid products shouldn't be available for those who prefer to have most or all of their expenses covered. That's a matter of individual or group choice, and is a model that we'll be exploring in more detail in Chapter 12 ("Insurance and Choice, Once Again"). But the pricing should reflect this level of coverage. The costs shouldn't be shifted to those who prefer a lower-cost product with higher deductibles.

Fee-for-Service an Incentive for Utilization

Most physicians and other caregivers are sincerely committed to providing the care that is appropriate for their patients. They're not motivated by greed. But they're paid for production; for doing things. In theory, payment methodologies compensate providers for *necessary* utilization. But there's often a certain imprecision and lack of consensus on just what is *necessary*.

Depending on how you measure, it's estimated that the costs for unnecessary health service utilization and waste is somewhere between 10% and 30% of total health care spending.[3] Even at the lower end of the scale at 10%, this translates into about $320 billion (!) that is being spent unnecessarily on health care.

There are, in fact, multiple reasons for the unnecessary utilization of services. But it doesn't take a Ph.D. in economics to understand the dynamics of a model where physicians and other caregivers are paid more for doing more, and are rewarded for recommending more complex interventions at times when a more conservative approach might be in order. As a result, the U.S. spends more on medical technologies of all kinds.

This more-is-better-than-less thinking is inculcated in physicians' education and training. Patients, as well, are often inclined to seek more costly interventions. Since neither the patient nor the physician typically suffers negative pocketbook consequences, there's little incentive to do otherwise.

On the flip side of this equation, there's an argument on the part of the medical profession that fee-for-service works in the best interest of patients, since fixed payment approaches may encourage providers to stint on services. There's a certain validity to this concern. But as will be discussed later, there are mechanisms that can be put in place to mitigate this problem.

Impact on Care Coordination

Providers are paid for performing discrete tasks. These tasks—micro-tasks, really—are tied to an arcane coding system that determines the level of payment for work performed. This greatly influences the course of evaluation and treatment. It encourages providers to do a lot of things on a solo basis when a more inter-disciplinary, team approach may be indicated. There's less incentive to take a holistic care approach, or worry too much about care coordination and transitions beyond the immediate scope of the caregiver's specific tasks. The provider operates a lot like a job-shop or assembly line worker, focusing on the task that is in front of them at that moment. But unlike an assembly line, there's often no overall systems engineer coordinating the overall flow of tasks from one worker to another.

The nature of medicine has changed. Unlike a previous era when most treatments were for specific, acute disorders, the requirements posed by chronic disease and multi-systemic disorders involve the combined efforts of multiple caregivers and disciplines. Health care is now a team sport. We need to bring our payment system into this new world, where caregivers are rewarded for team effort and have the incentives to optimize care through the full continuum. Paying physicians to work independently on a fee-for-service basis undermines this overall direction.

Care is further fragmented and depersonalized by the fact that electronic health records (EHRs) are used by caregivers to optimize fee-for-service payments. You have doubtlessly noticed in your own personal experiences how this has affected physician behaviors. They spend a lot of time pointing and clicking and making copious notes so that they have the right information loaded into the EHR. They're not trying to be rude or off-putting. That's just how they get paid.

A Recipe for Waste, Fraud, and Abuse

Health care providers and payers have deep layers of overhead and administrative costs that fall under the category of *billing and insurance-related* (BIR) functions. For providers, such functions include filing claims, prior authorizations, and performing various tasks related to managed care administration. Payer and third-party administrator BIR costs are largely billing-related.

The impact of BIR activities on the overall delivery system cost structure can't be overstated. For hospitals and doctors' offices, such costs account for *over one-half* of total administrative costs, and can be 10% or more of total revenue. It's been estimated that a simplified payer system in the U.S. could save over $350 billion annually. That's nearly 15% of the total amount spent on health care.[4]

Then there's the overpricing problem. This form of waste occurs when a given service or technology carries a price tag that is out of sync with any realistic cost basis and/or is delivered in a market where comparable services are delivered at a much lower cost. In almost any other industry the forces of a competitive market would remedy this situation. In health care, however, the usual market signals have historically been missing. For most consumers in most situations, there has been no market basket that could be used to compare and evaluate the price of a given health care *product*. Even now, the product value isn't at all tangible. It's an amalgamation of coded items and sub-items that lack any real meaning to the average person. But most of us accept this lack of transparency, simply because someone else is picking up most of the tab. We're largely shielded by third parties from the direct consequences of an artificially high price.

Payments for wasteful, fraudulent, and abuse claims, otherwise referred to as *improper payments*, are huge. Improper payments cover a broad category of ills. They include overpayments and payments that should not be made, payments to ineligible recipients, or payments for unnecessary services. Abuse occurs when a provider party intentionally misrepresents services provided. When you add the categories of estimated overutilization and inefficiently delivered services, the total of what could be considered unnecessary expenditures has historically been close to 45% of total health care outlays in the U.S. (Figure 4.1).

Unscrupulous providers can easily scam the system. Most commonly, providers *up-code* for services performed by billing for a service that is more costly than the one actually performed, or for a covered service when the actual service performed is not in a covered category. People can falsely claim to be providers, using illegitimate addresses and provider numbers.

Patients can perpetrate fraud as well. Addicts, for example, may see multiple providers and alter prescriptions to obtain drugs for personal use or to illegally sell on the street.

Medicare and Medicaid are the prime targets for fraudsters State Medicaid programs are notoriously lax when it comes to safeguards, and are rife with fraud in many states.

There are also built-in conflicts of interest for physicians. Physicians in some instances receive payment for not only the services that they provide directly, but also share in the profits of diagnostic and treatment facilities where they have

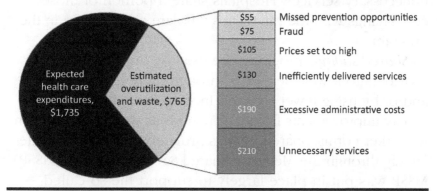

Figure 4.1   Health care overutilization and waste in the U.S. (dollars in billions). (From Institute of Medicine, 2012.)

ownership. Concerned about this *double-dipping*, Congress passed an amendment to the Social Security Act to prevent physicians from referring Medicare business to entities in which they have financial ownership. Commonly referred to as the Stark law, these provisions have mitigated certain abuses. But as we'll get into later, the Stark law has created its own set of problems, and has actually been a roadblock to more seamless care coordination in an era of value-based payment.

Moving toward Value

The industry is moving, at long last, in the direction of value-based reimbursement methodologies. Alternative payment models (APMs) are leading the way. APMs have a common objective, which is to connect provider reimbursement to measures of performance and outcomes. They come in several flavors, primarily variations of gainsharing, shared savings, bundled payment, and capitation models.

Gainsharing consists of payments by hospitals to participating physicians based on meeting targets designed to reduce costs and increase the quality of care. Gainsharing programs are largely targeted toward reducing costs of inpatient care through efficiencies at the point of service and by eliminating unnecessary services. Hospitals share a portion of those cost savings with the physicians who are participating in the program.

Shared savings programs are used by insurers to get providers to lower their costs through more efficient care and/or by using fewer services. Incentives are based on cost/quality improvements from past periods as well as comparisons to market norms. Shared savings programs have come to life largely through the Medicare Shared Savings Program (MSSP). MSSP was put in place largely to support the so-called Accountable Care Organizations (ACOs) that were developed as part of the ACA implementation. The concept of MSSP is to take providers toward risk-based contracts where their payment levels are based in part on meeting certain quality and cost targets. Various levels of downside/upside risk (track levels) are incorporated in the program, whereby providers get a portion of the overall savings for a defined patient population, or share in the downside if targets are not met. The intent has been to push providers toward the more advanced models where their risk for monetary loss is substantial enough to significantly affect clinical behavior.

There are limitations to both the gainsharing and shared savings models. One is what you might call the *half-life* issue. That is to say that once certain targets are met, what's next? Do you lower the cost targets again? At what point are you encouraging physicians to cut corners and reduce service utilization in a way that is actually detrimental to patient care? And there are related legal problems if there's no objective way of verifying cost savings, or if quality indicators are questionable in any way.

The other limitation of pay-for-performance programs is that they're designed to work within the framework of a traditional provider setting, which is to say they are focused on discrete, narrowly-defined services. They don't provide incentives for care coordination through the full service continuum.

In order for shared savings models such as ACOs to be successful, they've got to make economic sense on both the payer and provider sides of the equation. This involves the assumption of significant downside as well as upside risk. This, in turn, begs the question of whether you can seriously manage the risk equation with a model that depends on the alignment and teamwork of players in disparate organizations that have their own vested interests and economic obligations to stakeholders and creditors. As we'll cover in Chapter 7 ("Where's the Competition?"), the same government that's encouraging inter-provider cooperation is giving mixed signals when it comes to provider partnerships and true integration. For these reasons, one could question whether ACO-type models are viable constructs over the long term.

Some of the earlier limitations are at least partly addressed in the *bundled payment* model. In this model providers are paid for an overall care episode, typically an inpatient stay. In many respects it's a mid-zone between traditional fee-for-service and capitation, discussed below. The distinction between bundled payment and more traditional methodologies is that it starts to get away from the old *pay-for-doing* approach. An extremely important feature of this methodology is that it incentivizes providers to coordinate efforts to maximize value. It gives both purchasers and consumers a known price point. Definitely a move in the right direction!

But bundled payment also has its drawbacks. Some types of illnesses or disorders don't fall neatly into definable *episodes*. Another concern expressed by some of my academic colleagues is that this payment method can disadvantage research applications and new patient care technologies.

The *capitation* payment method is at the exact opposite end of the spectrum from the traditional fee-for-service model. Under capitation, insurers pay fixed monthly amounts to providers or provider networks for each subscriber. It's then up to the caregivers to provide needed services to the subscriber population within this fixed dollar amount.

There are essentially two variations of capitation. One is *global capitation*, where all services are covered and the plan essentially assumes the actuarial risk of its enrolled population. The other is *partial capitation*, where a core group of services are provided under a single payment provision, and other services are provided on a fee-for-service basis.

A principal advantage of capitation is that it gives health systems the incentive to provide the most cost-effective care through the full care cycle. This may entail the use of care pathways or technologies that would not necessarily maximize revenues under the traditional fee-for-service approach. In other words, it gives caregivers the ability to rationalize care and use resources in the most clinically- and cost-effective fashion. Capitation bypasses all the red tape and complexities of the typical fee-for-service billing and payment methodology. And it gives the health system a predictable revenue flow that can be built right into the overall budget.

Is capitation the answer? I believe that it's a model that can be attractive and work well for certain population segments. But it's not a model that is necessarily suitable for everyone, and there are some inherent drawbacks. For one thing, it can restrict patients' choice of providers. The market's experiences with HMO gatekeeper models in the 1990s should serve to remind us that people are loath to give up their ability to choose doctors and hospitals. It can also lead to stinting on care processes in some instances. Direct accountability on the part of individual caregivers is often lacking. There are often no or limited provisions built into the model related to preventive health care and health status improvement for the subscriber population.

Problems Measuring Value

The various alternative payment models described earlier are a major step forward. But for the most part we're looking at somewhat artificial measures of costs. *The way that health care institutions are organized—and the manner in which costs and outcomes are measured—make it difficult to track, let alone deliver, value.* Individual providers and departments measure discrete services, but don't necessarily have a way of evaluating the relationships of inputs to outcomes and value. Costs are typically looked at as *billing units* at a departmental or cost center level, as opposed to being considered from an episode of care perspective. Thus, individual physicians and other service providers may not feel a direct responsibility for outcomes, nor are there incentives for the caregivers to assume joint responsibility.

The industry is also challenged in its ability to directly link quality measures to value. *Currently, quality measures focus mostly on inputs rather than outputs.* The Healthcare Effectiveness Data and Information Set (HEDIS) indicators are mostly all process measures. They're useful, to be sure. But they don't look at care delivery and outcomes from an overall, systemic standpoint. Performance improvement tends to focus on discrete service components, often missing the opportunities for improved processes and throughput across the total care cycle. This means that there's no shared accountability for the overall product. And perhaps more important, the organization is lacking the complete feedback loop that is critical to organizational learning and process improvement.

Another problem with certain value-based formulas is that they tend to treat patient populations much the same. This can unfairly advantage or disadvantage certain caregivers, depending on the types of patients they are seeing. A recent study found that Medicare's value-based modifiers put doctors who treat sicker, low income patients at a disadvantage, while skewing bonus payments toward those who have healthier, higher-income patients.[5]

Providers need to look at value and share in the accountability for outcomes from a system-wide perspective. This begs the question, "What's the end-stage product?" Increasingly, the product can't be defined as a single-stage intervention, but must be considered on a longitudinal basis, and be measured in terms of recovery and the sustainability of improved health status.

An underlying dynamic that affects any relevant reform of health plan design is that the very nature of medical risk is changing. Going back in time, medical risk was more of a function of random and somewhat infrequent events; for example, contagious disease, genetic conditions, or automobile accidents. Now conditions are more related to predictable chronic diseases, as well as various behavioral, substance abuse, and environmental factors. Many of the treatments and costs associated with the current risk profiles are preventable, or can be mitigated through early detection and treatment. But health plan designs are still for the most part stuck in time, with a high level of coverage for acute interventions (many of which are discretionary) but little or no coverage for preventative services that could substantially reduce the long-term costs of care.

And whereas physicians are paid for services related to the treatment of an illness or injury, they're not necessarily reimbursed for preventive care or consultations that aren't connected to an episode of care. Ironically, both doctors and patients are often *fully* covered for expensive discretionary services that are not threatening to life or health.

In the final analysis, the need to change how we pay providers for delivering health care is not just about the money. It's about the quality and effectiveness of medicine. It determines when and how care is delivered. We need to move toward reimbursement models that reward timely intervention, the most clinically efficacious use of technologies, and true teamwork among caregivers throughout the full care cycle.

References

1. M. J. Perry, *Why are Health Care Costs So High?* American Enterprise Institute, June 18, 2013, Washington, DC.
2. R. H. Brooks et al., The effects of co-insurance on the health of adults. Results from the RAND Health Insurance Experiment, RAND Corporation, 1984. Report R-3055-HHS, Santa Monica, CA.
3. S. Brownlee, V. Saini, and C. Cassel, When less is more: Issues of overuse in health care, *Health Affairs Blog Post*, April 25, 2014. doi:10.1377/hblog20140425.038647.
4. A. Jiwani et al., Billing and insurance-related administrative costs in United States Healthcare, *BMC Health Services Research*, abstract, November 13, 2014, p. 1.
5. J. Commins, Value-based payments must address patient mix, *Media Health Leaders*, December 5, 2017.

Chapter 5

Silos, Everywhere

sys·tem, n.

1. A regularly interacting or independent group of items forming a unified whole
2. An organized or established procedure

—Merriam-Webster Dictionary

CHAPTER OVERVIEW

- The concept of *system* is still missing in much of health care.
- Service fragmentation is a pervasive industry problem.
- Provider-to-provider coordination is often lacking, even within the same organization.
- Information silos contribute to the fragmentation problem.
- There's a gap between sick care, well care, and population health.
- The silo mentality is embedded in the industry DNA.

Automobiles Get Pretty Good Health Care...

On a recent business trip my BMW started to lurch badly upon acceleration. Close to 200 miles from home base, I was able to navigate to a dealership located several miles down the road. A service coordinator took my key fob. Using its code, he was able to retrieve the car's history—it's *electronic health record*—within seconds: where purchased, when serviced, services performed, past problems, and so on. The vehicle was then hooked up to a diagnostic scanner, which quickly determined that the problem was residual pressure in a fuel line.

Thirty minutes later everything was fixed and I was on my way. All under warranty. As I left the dealership, the service coordinator reminded me that it was time to get the car in for routine inspection and maintenance. "Just good to prevent future problems," he said. "And it's covered in your maintenance program. No extra charges."

As I drove away I began to play out in my mind how this experience might have gone if the auto service business was structured in a manner similar to health care. I would stop at the dealer's *urgent care center* (service department). After an obligatory lengthy wait—during which time I would be sharing detailed vehicle information and service history with a desk clerk—a technician would take the vehicle out for a brief drive to get a sense of the problem. Upon return he would confirm the car is indeed lurching upon acceleration. "So what do you think the problem is?" I would ask. "Not sure," he would reply. "Could be fuel injection system, or maybe the transmission. Or maybe it's the engine management system. You'll need to get evaluations from specialists in each of those areas. They each run their own tests. You'll need to figure out which technicians you want to use and set up the appointments."

"So," I ask, "how much will this cost? Will it be covered by my warranty?" "Can't answer that question," he responds. "We'll just have to see what the problem is. But the technicians probably won't be able to predict what their costs are going to be. You see, there may be different ways to fix the problem and each tech has their own way of doing things. They each bill for their own time and parts. And they can't be sure of what the components will actually cost, since they're sourced from various vendors who set their own prices. You'll just have to wait until you get your bill to see what it all comes to."

"By the way," he adds, "I see that you're from out of state. Unfortunately your warranty doesn't cover you here, since it only applies to dealers in your own home state. You know, state regulations."

Hardly a seamless, customer-friendly experience. It's hard to imagine any successful business model that could operate this way. Where the consumer needs a product, but must personally navigate through a maze of producers and vendors to piece the product together, and do all of this with little information about the quality and value of the various components, let alone what the finished product will cost.

Welcome to health care. When it comes to how we interact with the business of medicine we're a lot like the hapless car owner in my scenario. We can't always predict what services we will need or when they will be needed. As consumers/patients, we have limited knowledge about the clinical nature of our problems or the appropriate remedies. We're often in a position of having to choose providers, set up appointments, and make all of the various logistical decisions necessary to navigate highly complex systems. The process can be very impersonal. We know that costs are likely to be outrageously high, but we have no control over them, and don't know what they'll be until we're presented with the final bill.

Even if we have insurance coverage, we often don't know what our portion of the tab will be—what our *out of warranty* costs will be.

Where's the "System" in Health Care?

We use the word *system* loosely in health care. We sometimes refer to the U.S. health care system. Health care provider organizations typically identify themselves as systems. There are disease management systems, patient care management systems, information systems, and the list goes on.

But anyone who has had any involvement with U.S. health care at any level understands that there is little that fits the definition of a system as "a regularly interacting or independent group of items forming a unified whole." What we have is more of a collection of silos—parts bins of services incorporating various disciplines, technologies, provider organizations, stages of care, modalities, third party payers and regulators.

Table 5.1 provides a quick snapshot of some of the major categories of caregivers, types and stages of care, and provider organizations:

This is just a high-level profile. If you take it to a more granular level, there are more types of organizations, professionals, and levels of care than you can count. For example, the AMA Masterfile alone lists 45 specialty groupings and over 200 specialty categories. In addition, we have a mind-boggling array of nursing and allied health disciplines and sub-disciplines licensed as separate categories.

Each of these segments has its own distinct focus and culture. Not to mention vested interests that tend protect the agenda and sanctity of each silo. There's a natural motivation on the part of each professional and provider

Table 5.1 Health Care Delivery Segments

Care Stages/Modalities	Caregiver Disciplines	Provider Organizations
Disease prevention	Primary care physicians	Physician practices/ Groups
Primary care	Physician specialists	Independent practice Associations
Secondary care	Registered nurses	Hospitals/Health systems
Tertiary acute care	Licensed practical nurses	Academic health centers
Quaternary care	Clinical nursing specialists	Ambulatory surgery centers
Chronic disease treatment	Physician assistants	Retail clinics
Chronic disease management	Certified nurse midwives	Home care agencies
Inpatient care	Mental health professionals	Long-term care facilities
Outpatient care	Dentists and oral care practitioners	Rehabilitation facilities
Home health care	Physical therapists	Hospices
Rehabilitative care	Speech therapists	Health maintenance organizations
Long-term care	Occupational health professionals	Preferred provider organizations
Palliative care	Public health professionals	Managed care organizations
Etc.	Home health care professionals	Accountable care organizations
	Geriatric care professionals	Clinically integrated networks
	Etc.	Etc.

organization to do a particular thing. This becomes the lens through which they see patients, problems, and solutions.

The Problems of Service Fragmentation

Health care wasn't always this complex. Going back to the early part of the eighteenth century, health care consisted of various home remedies and itinerant doctors with little science-based training. This changed dramatically when it was discovered that those things called *germs* caused disease, giving rise to the development of medical science, technology, and the proliferation of caregiver professions. Without question this evolution toward specialized medicine has made enormous contributions to the effective treatment of disease. But there are some pitfalls of putting so much emphasis on specialty care.

In the twenty-first century health care processes are seldom centered on a single diagnosis or condition. This is increasingly the case as the number of patients with multiple chronic conditions continues to grow. As discussed in Chapter 2, our aging population as well as other high-risk populations often have one or more conditions that may involve more than one physical illness. In addition, many of these patients have an overlay of behavioral conditions: mental illness, substance abuse, cognitive impairment disorders, and developmental disabilities. With chronic disease, there's often a need to shift the focus of treatment from one of strictly *cure* to that of dealing with the effects of long-term illness and handicap. This requires an interdisciplinary team approach that involves not only the relevant physicians, but also nurses at various levels, physician assistants, pharmacists, nutritionists, physical therapists, social workers, mental health professionals, patient navigators, and so on.

Patients today, particularly those with co-morbidities, are almost invariably cared for by multiple providers. Studies have determined that the median Medicare patient, for example, sees *seven* doctors in four different practices over the course of a year.[1] Although each physician may have an important role and provide high-quality care, they don't always have the time or make the effort to coordinate with one another. The challenge often falls to the patient or family members to navigate the confusing pathways between caregivers, stages of care, and care settings. This can be especially problematic in the common instance where patients are transferred from one institution to another—say, from a hospital to a rehabilitation center.

Even within the same health care system, processes often vary between primary care and specialty providers. Patients are often unclear as to why they're being referred to a given speciality physicans, or how to navigate the care process after being seen by a specialist. Specialists, in turn, don't always receive adequate information regarding the reasons for a referral, or have the up-to-date information from tests that have already been conducted.

Studies show that *many if not most medical errors occur due to a lack of teamwork coordination* and effective data sharing between caregivers within a given hospital or other health care setting. And despite the positive effect of care coordination on overall outcomes and costs, insurance companies don't typically pay doctors for the time spent in doing so.

Clinical pathways are a principal means of managing the quality of health care through the standardization of care processes. These processes are ideally established through evidence-based practices. It seems like such a basic concept. But well-defined clinical pathways are often absent. Or if they exist, they are in many instances applied to a single stage of treatment (e.g., acute intervention). For patients requiring multiple disciplines and stages of care, there's often a lack of service coordination across the care and time continuum.

Information Silos: Part of the Problem

Interoperability is an impressive-sounding word used to describe the ability of disparate information systems to communicate with one another, exchange data, and then use the information that has been exchanged. Despite a lot of time and dollars spent on this challenge in recent years, we still don't have a lot of interoperability between our various heath care provider information systems.

A typical patient care experience can easily involve two or more physicians, laboratory and pharmacy services, therapists, and multiple modalities and sites. Payers are part of the process chain as well. While there's a compelling need for connectivity between all the players in a given treatment sequence, the relevant patient data are often still sequestered in information silos. This is despite the fact that we have the technological means to connect networks and free up the flow of information.

Many physicians still don't have fully functional electronic medical information systems. Even if they do, their records are often incompatible with or do not interconnect with others. Unless they're being treated within a highly integrated health system, the patients themselves may have to acquire and keep track of medical records and test results, and see that all the caregivers that they are dealing with have access to those records. Otherwise tests may be unnecessarily duplicated, or worse, may simply fall between the cracks, posing unnecessary risks to the patient.

There are multiple reasons for this seeming inability to achieve greater interoperability. Many health care providers still have home-grown and legacy information platforms that are of a closed design. Plus, believe it or not, there are still a lot of caregivers who are reluctant to convert from traditional paper-based records to electronic systems.

The Health Information Technology for Economic and Clinical Health Act, or HITECH Act for short, was passed in 2010 with the intent of accelerating both the creation and sharing of patient-based electronic health records (EHRs) between health care providers. Among other things, HITECH also directed that patients be given access to their own health records in an electronic format. (Can you believe it? We can now have access to our *own* files!)

Huge dollars have been spent by the U.S. government to incent hospitals and health professionals to *meaningfully use* electronic health records and participate in health information exchanges. *But just a small percentage of health care systems are actually sharing data electronically.* And even fewer doctors' offices. This is despite the overwhelming evidence that the sharing of electronic information plays such an important role in influencing the quality, cost, and overall experience of patient care.

Another obstacle to the smooth flow of patient information exchange has to do with the motivation of some providers and insurance companies to maintain proprietary control over information (and implicitly, control over the patient). On top of this, there are the problems of restrictive and often conflicting state laws that pose information barriers for patients who have providers located in different states.

To help overcome these roadblocks, states were encouraged under the HITECH Act to fund so-called Health Information Exchanges (HIEs) for the purpose of exchanging patient-centric health information between provider organizations at the point of care. Although there has been fairly broad provider participation in HIEs, the future prospects of the model will depend on long-term funding and whether or not the market sees enough value to backfill the funding gaps that will occur as government subsidies wind down. In the final analysis, there'll need to be an alignment of incentives between providers and insurance companies to justify the cost of footing the HIE bill over the long-term. The jury's out on this.

The barriers to interoperability aren't technological. They're man-made. We can solve these problems, but need to get past the proprietary and cultural roadblocks.

Geographic Silos, Too

One would think that through the sharing of data and evidence-based best practices, there would be a growing standardization of care processes and results from one geographic area to another. But studies continue to point to significantly different approaches and corresponding variations in clinical and cost outcomes by region of the country. Such variations have been extensively documented and studied by the Dartmouth research team. Published in the Dartmouth Atlas, the research shows more than a two-fold variation in per capita spending in different regions of the country. The Dartmouth researchers have discovered huge differences in medical practice that have significant implications for patient care and related costs.[2]

One of the most significant findings of the Dartmouth research has been the identification of a benchmark for spending that provides a relevant measure of the level of unnecessary costs, otherwise known as waste. By comparing various regions to low-spending regions and adjusting for certain quality variables, it's been estimated that we could achieve savings in the range of 20%–30% with no adverse effect on outcomes.[2]

Population Health: More Teamwork Needed

One of the most positive aspects of the Affordable Care Act has been to put the spotlight on population health. Among other things, there's been recognition that the management of health care costs is ultimately related to provisions for prevention, early detection, and disease management. An entire health industry sub-culture has subsequently evolved around the whole concept of population health.

The goals of population health are laudable. And it seems that this initiative by its very nature would tend to bring together caregivers, institutions, and professional disciplines into a team framework. But ironically, what I have observed in my own work is that there's often a virtual disconnect between the services provided in the private, acute care sector and those provided by public health agencies. There's frequently a lack of inter-agency cooperation at the community level in terms of setting priorities and aligning efforts targeted toward prevention and health status improvement. And there's little care coordination and sharing of clinical and patient information in the many instances where patients are being treated in both private institutional and public agency settings.

One of the main stumbling blocks to population health initiatives has been what some have referred to as the *medicalization* of public health issues. The problem is that there has been a tendency to make access to traditional medicine an overarching goal, when the root problems have more to do with social and economic issues related to education, income, lifestyle, housing, availability of healthy foods, lifestyle, substance abuse, and so on.

Another obstacle goes back to the tendency of the health care industry to fragment into professional sub-cultures. Many health care professionals who believe they are on the cutting edge of population health have taken a somewhat standoffish attitude toward more traditional medicine. At the same time, many in the more established medical disciplines view population health as "something else" and not within the mainstream of medicine.

Silo Culture Part of the Industry's DNA

The identified need for more coordinated care models is not a new concept. In its 2001 groundbreaking report, "Crossing the Quality Chasm: A New Health System for the Twenty-First Century," the Institute of Medicine (IOM) documented the common situation where patients receiving care for one chronic condition were not necessarily receiving any attention for other unrelated conditions. The IOM cautioned strongly against defining patients on the basis of a single disease or condition, and designing care models on the basis of specific conditions.[3]

As a result of my own work with health systems in designing and implementing integrated delivery platforms, I'm fully aware of the challenges of putting together well-functioning interdisciplinary teams. There are typically clinical turf issues involved, as well as differing professional cultures, values, incentives, and priorities. Clinical departments are by nature very hierarchal, and there's often a resistance to accepting a new structure that changes the traditional flow of authority.

The seeds of professional silos are planted in the education and training of health care professionals. Each discipline has its own theoretical filter through which people perceive, analyse, and address patient problems. In his highly recognized research on this topic, Dr. Hugh Petrie refers to this as the professional's *cognitive map*. Petrie observes that "...quite literally, two opposing disciplinarians can look at the same thing and not see the same thing."[4] This adds to the whole communications and coordination challenge between not only the caregivers and patients, but between the caregivers themselves.

There are literally hundreds of organizations, agencies, societies, and advocacy groups that influence, oversee, or represent a vast array of industry and consumer segments. A partial listing of such organizations is provided in Table 5.2. These various industry disciplines, groups, and sub-groups have their own identities and cultures.

Some of these organizations and agencies fulfill important roles in ensuring the safety and quality of health care in the U.S. But many of them have redundant, overlapping, or conflicting agendas. They represent the interests of their respective constituency groups. But who's looking out for the patient? The patient is the most vulnerable, but arguably the least represented, segment of all.

Table 5.2 Third-Party and Influencing Organizations

Health Plans/Payers (examples)	Licensure & Regulatory Bodies (examples)	Associations, Societies, Trade Organizations (examples)
Commercial insurance plans	Physician and Allied Health Licensure Bodies	American Medical Association
Blue Cross Blue Shield Assn. Plans	Joint Commission on Accreditation of Healthcare Organizations	American Osteopathic Association
Employer-based health plans	Centers for Medicare and Medicaid Services	American Hospital Association
Individual/Family plans	Health Insurance Portability and Accountability Act (HIPAA)	Federation of American Hospitals
HMOs	U.S. Dep't. of Health and Human Services (HHS)	American Nursing Association
PPOs	State Insurance Regulators	American Dental Association
Medicare	State Certificate of Need Agencies	American Health Lawyers Association
Medicaid	Federal Trade Commission	American Pharmacists Association
Qualified plans	Office of the Nat'l. Coordinator for Health Information Technology	American Psychiatric Association
Medical savings accounts	Food and Drug Administration	American Health Insurance Plans

(Continued)

Table 5.2 (*Continued*)   Third-Party and Influencing Organizations

Health Plans/Payers (examples)	Licensure & Regulatory Bodies (examples)	Associations, Societies, Trade Organizations (examples)
CHAMPUS	Patent and Trademark Office	Association of American
Veteran's Affairs Plans	Etc.	Medical Colleges
State Children's Health Insurance		Professional Societies and Colleges (many
Catastrophic Plans		State Hospital Associations
Admin. Services Only Payers		State Medical Associations
Etc.		National Patient Advocacy Org.
		National Assn. of Manufacturers
		Etc.

As we consider how to breach the silo walls, it's important to understand that the existing players—whether providers, payers, or overseers—have strong vested interests in preserving their respective turfs. Many have long-standing membership in the MAC enterprise. We may hear all the politically correct verbiage about improving patient care, eliminating waste, and focusing on prevention and population health. But many of the industry constituents who need to make the needed changes are pretty comfortable with the way things are.

References

1. H. Hoangmai et al., Primary care physicians' links to other physicians through medicare patients: The scope of care coordination, *Annals of Internal Medicine*, 150(4): 236–242, 2009.
2. J. Skinner, E. S. Fisher, *Reflections on Geographic Variations in Health Care*, The Dartmouth Institute for Health Policy and Clinical Practice, Lebanon, NH, March 31, 2010.
3. Crossing the Quality Chasm: A New Health System for the 21st Century, Institute of Medicine (US) Committee on Quality of Health Care in America. National Academies Press, Washington, DC, 2001.
4. H. G. Petrie, Do you see what I see? The epistemology of interdisciplinary inquiry, *Educational Researcher*, 5(2): 9–15, 1976.

Chapter 6

The Real Costs of Regulation

"If there is any lesson in the history of ideas, it is that good intentions tell you nothing about the actual consequences."

—Thomas Sowell, Economist

CHAPTER OVERVIEW

- Regulations micromanage the business of medicine.
- Pricing regulations have actually made prices higher.
- Certificate-of-Need restricts competition and protects industry insiders.
- Unnecessary regulations slow innovation and progress.
- Malpractice liability laws lead to higher health care costs.
- The real costs of regulatory overreach are the negative impacts on industry and market functionality.

The Perils of Regulatory Overreach

Have you been injured by a turtle lately? Let's see, that's code W5922XA. Or maybe by a sea lion? Different code. That would be W5612XA. Seriously, these are real codes! Or perhaps you've been burned by flaming water skis. Have to look that one up, but yes, it's got a code, too.

The newly-implemented International Classification of Diseases version 10 (ICD10) has a total of 141,060 (yes, you read that correctly) code sets used to record and report medical diagnoses and inpatient procedures. If you're wondering why your physician may seem preoccupied with things other than the patient sitting in front of her, this is but one example of how rules and regulations have invaded the day-to-day practice of medicine.

Health care regulations at federal, state, and local levels have metastasized to a level where they exert control over virtually every aspect of health care delivery. Although some regulations have to do with safety standards, a huge number of them are really oriented more to the business of health care. They tell us what services will be available to us, where and how they should be delivered, and how much we should pay for them.

Yes, we need to have regulations in health care. They are necessary because they help to protect patients from harm and provide safeguards against fraud and abuse. But there's an implicit premise that regulators know more about health care than the caregivers themselves. That's where things go off course.

Regulations are all about compliance, not results. But sometimes compliance can lead to unintended consequences. The penalty on Medicare patient readmissions is an example of the perils of regulatory overreach. Medicare has designed their readmission reduction program with a focus on 30-day readmissions. There are financial penalties of up to 3% of a hospital's Medicare dollars if its readmission levels exceed the guidelines. Hospital stays account for about a third of the national health care tab. So it makes sense to avoid the need to readmit patients for a given condition, right?

Except when it doesn't. According to a recent study, an estimated 10,000 heart failure patients may be dying unnecessarily every year because of incentives to keep them out of the hospital.[1] What the study found is that there are pressures on providers to err on the side of *not* admitting patients in situations where they may be subject to the penalty. So, for example, there might be a tendency to not readmit a heart patient discharged 20 days ago when his or her condition indicates that readmission might be safer.

By way of comparison, the penalty for exceeding mortality rate guidelines is only 0.2% of revenue dollars—a small fraction of the readmission hit. Apparently compliance is more important than keeping people alive!

The Computer Will See You Now

You may recall a time when your physician dictated the results of an exam and a transcriptionist entered the details into a medical record. Each subsequent visit built on that record, and a detailed patient history was created. Sitting in the doctor's exam room, you felt like you had his full attention. Now this same doctor is spending a significant portion of his time staring at a computer screen and making real-time data entries.

Electronic health record (EHR) systems were intended to improve treatment efficiency and accuracy. But the reality has been one of mixed results. Electronic health records are not always the most accurate. When a physician enters a patient's medical number the history of that person's medications, tests, and procedures comes up in a checkbox format. The doctor is then able to click selected boxes to note what was done during the visit. But the entry is in a structured format of data choices, and none of the choices may fit the exact circumstances of that particular patient. So the actual entry may be a *best fit* approximation. But it isn't always an accurate reflection of the patient's specific situation. The EHR algorithm may encourage a doctor to use a certain medication, or not to order certain tests. This can improve time and cost efficiency, but can also be a case of misdirection when the circumstances of a given patient deviate from empirical norms.

The role of computer technology in patient care was greatly expanded by the aforementioned HITECH Act. HITECH was intended to promote the role of the computer in patient care, and set forth standardized requirements for the types of data that must be collected from patients. In addition, CMS put in place so-called *meaningful use* rules. These rules gave physicians incentives to use certified EHR technology to "improve quality, safety, efficiency, and reduce health disparities."

The meaningful use provisions were transitioned to a successor program as part of the Medicare Access and Children's Health Insurance Program (CHIP) Reauthorization Act of 2015 (MACRA). MACRA now manages the practice of medicine down to the minute detail. In a recent *Wall Street Journal* article, James Capretta at the American Enterprise Institute and Lanhee Chen at the Hoover Institution put it bluntly: "MACRA adopts the same theory of cost control embedded in Obamacare. It assumes that the federal government has the knowledge and wherewithal to engineer better health care.... A better plan would use competition and consumer choice to reward physicians for providing high-quality care at affordable and easily ascertained prices, without coercion by the federal government."[2]

The question of EHR benefits versus costs has lingered throughout the process of implementation. Based on recent research jointly conducted by the RAND Corporation and American Medical Association (AMA), the majority of physicians have become very frustrated with the hassle and cost of a system that has yet to prove its worth in terms of efficiency and quality of care.[3] The lack of EHR user-friendliness, interoperability, and functionality top the list of frustrations. Plus, doctors who don't have scribes find themselves performing lower-skill level tasks that sub-optimize their work efforts and the time that could be spent on what they were trained to do.

A survey of physicians conducted by Medscape determined that only about a third of physicians believe that EHRs have a positive effect on patient encounters, while 70% indicate a negative impact on the quality of their face-to-face time with patients (Table 6.1).[4]

Table 6.1   Impact of EHRs on Patient Care

EHRs' Effect on Patient Encounters Survey Results from Physician Respondents[a]		
Positive Impact	35%	Improves my ability to respond to patient issues
	33%	Allows me to more effectively manage patient treatment plans
	10%	Allows me to spend more face-to-face time with patients
	9%	Allows me to see more patients
Negative Impact	70%	Decreases my face-to-face time with patients
	57%	Decreases my ability to see more patients
	27%	Decreases my ability to respond to patient issues
	26%	Decreases my ability to effective manage patient treatment plans

Source: L. Kane, N. Chesanow, *Medscape EHR Report 2014*, WebMD LLC, New York, pp. 18–19, July 15, 2014.

[a] Respondents could choose multiple answers.

The implementation of the new ICD10 patient disease classification scheme has added to the challenge of the doctor's daily routine. But even before the roll-out of the new codes, doctors were already spending about a third of their time in the patient exam room making data entries. According to a recent Northwestern University study, this is roughly three times the amount of time that physicians who use the old-fashioned payer charts spend looking at them.[5] This doesn't include all the physician time spent on such things as credentialing, pre-authorizations, quality data, formularies, claims, billing, and so on. Needless to say, this leaves proportionately less time available to attend to patients. This is a source of frustration and dissatisfaction for caregiver and patient alike.

The Price of Regulating Prices

Regulated pricing doesn't save money. Instead of supporting true competition, *pricing controls actually strengthen the monopoly power of existing providers.* They serve to obscure the true nature of costs and cost behavior.

Medicare sets a so-called *fair price* for every procedure and service. Under the traditional Medicare methodology, prices for hospital services are set using a base rate for a specified unit of service—one of the 140,000 diagnostic and procedure codes noted earlier. Adjustments are made based on factors related to geographic region, the patient's clinical severity, and certain other factors. Payment levels to physicians are based on a calculated fee schedule for over 7,000 services, known as the Resource-Based Relative Value Scale (RBRVS).

The problem is that Medicare prices don't necessarily reflect the actual costs of production, aren't always updated in a timely manner, and don't correlate to what the pricing would be in a truly competitive market. When you use administrative data and algorithms (and political influences) to set prices, you're inevitably going to be out of sync with what a true value-based price would be in a market-driven environment.

Medicare prices set the benchmarks for the private insurance market as well. This was recently documented in a study conducted by researchers at the University of California at San Diego. They analyzed millions of claims to look at the correlation between changes in Medicare prices for physician and outpatient services and the subsequent changes in the private market. "Our results indicate that the private sector will copy Medicare's pricing errors," stated Joshua Gottlieb, one of the researchers. Mr. Gottlieb went on to say that providers would actually be receiving higher payments overall if Medicare costs reflected the actual costs of production.[6] Other studies over recent years have corroborated this shadow pricing phenomenon.

Medicare pricing has a substantial impact on the individual hospital's financial stability. While Medicare dollars account for about 20% of total health care spending, they are over 45% of the average non-profit hospital's revenues. Medicare payment levels are typically sufficient to cover direct costs plus some contribution to overhead. But most Medicare reimbursement levels aren't profitable of and by themselves. This means that hospitals must find ways to offset this pricing structure. Medicare pricing, because of its artificially low level, has a negative impact on a hospital's ability to generate profit, accumulate capital, and make investments in response to community needs. No margin, no mission. As will be discussed later, this reality throws some cold water on the arguments of those who believe that *Medicare for all* is the answer we're looking for.

There have been and will continue to be political pressures to impose stringent pricing regulations on all sectors of health care as a means of harnessing the rising cost of care. But proponents of such measures ignore the history of failure of regulated pricing in other countries, which is the cause of systemic service shortages, negative impacts on access and quality, and yes, higher costs. Stringent pricing controls in Japan, for example, have resulted in these unhappy outcomes. The Netherlands was headed down the same path, and has now reinstated market-based pricing. Closer to home, the State of Maryland, which has had a government bureaucracy in place for years to set hospital prices, has found that it has only succeeded in giving more power to providers and actually inflating prices.[7] All of our experience to date suggests that any future efforts to micro-manage health care pricing will create more problems than they will solve.

Certificate of Need a CON Job

Let's say that you have a *proof of need* law in your local community that determines who can open up a new retail establishment such as a coffee shop or grocery store. Let's further say that the process involves a public hearing whereby existing retailers are allowed to comment on whether or not a new establishment is needed. "No, the community already has a coffee shop. Don't need another." Or imagine if someone wants to start an Airbnb. Since local hotels are not fully occupied, permission is denied.

The above scenarios are literally the situation in health care in states where Certificate of Need (CON) laws still exist. The National Health Planning and Resources Development Act (aka Comprehensive Health Planning, CHP) was passed by Congress in 1974 to deal with the rapid and oft-times unwarranted hospital expansion that was occurring at the time. Much of this construction was due to the stimulus of another government program, the Hospital Survey and Construction Act, otherwise known as Hill–Burton. This infusion of funding, combined with a *cost-plus* reimbursement formula (cost of operations plus cost of capital), was a sure-fire recipe for overbuilding. To counter this, state agencies were set up under the CHP legislation to review proposed capital projects, and issue certificates-of-need for hospital expansions or new services that were deemed consistent with *community need.*

The original rationale for CON no longer exists. The Hill–Burton program was discontinued in 1980. Then the introduction of the prospective payment system (PPS) took the industry away from the *a-dollar-spent-is-a-dollar-plus-reimbursed* mind-set. Depending on the size and type of institution, fixed costs can account for more than 80% of a hospital's total costs. So, having facility capacity and technology that is appropriately sized to market demand and that is efficiently utilized, is critical to having sound financial operations. If hospitals misjudge these factors and overbuild, the standing costs will put them under. There's a powerful economic incentive to have the right services and capacities in place.

Recognizing that the primary mission of CHP was no longer relevant, Congress rescinded the CON mandate in 1986. But 35 states still have some form of Certificate of Need. Why is this? There are multiple reasons. One has to do with the fundamental difficulty of decommissioning *any* public agency for any reason. As Ronald Reagan famously said, "A government bureau is the nearest thing to eternal life we'll ever see...."

But there's another reason. The CON process has been co-opted by industry interests. Health systems, like any other business, have incentives to protect their turf and block new entrants whenever possible. The planning boards that make the approval decisions at the state agencies are political appointees. They have ties to the communities involved and are often prone to make decisions that favor entrenched interests. *Certificate of Need has, in effect, become a franchise protection program.*

If I sound a bit cynical, it's because I have been directly and indirectly involved in many of these proceedings throughout the country. I have witnessed first-hand how politics and special interests have trumped objective criteria. The system became so corrupt in my home state of Illinois that my firm took the position many years ago of declining any requests for CON consulting or advocacy assistance in that state. You literally could not be successful on behalf of a client organization without under-the-table dealings with people in the business of peddling influence. It was that bad.

Certificate of Need laws need to be repealed. State planning agencies should be disbanded. That's not just my opinion. For years there has been a bipartisan consensus at the Federal Trade Commission that this form of regulation should be done away with, and that existing CON laws essentially exist to serve vested industry interests.[8]

More Regulation, Less Innovation

The good news is that the U.S. arguably produces more break-through drugs and biomedical technology than any other nation. It's not that we necessarily have a monopoly on talent or innovative skills. It's just that we have a patent system that protects the inventor in ways and for lengths of time that ensure that a successful product will generate a substantial return on investment. This attracts inventors and entrepreneurs from all over the world.

The bad news is that our system of patent protection is under constant attack, and is in danger of being changed in ways that would discourage invention and investment. Companies in the drug and device industry, especially the pharmaceutical business, have a high percentage of new product development failures. The pricing and related profit margins of the products that are successful must be at a level to compensate for this risk and reward stockholders, and at the same time support ongoing research and development.

Recurring proposals to curtail *profiteering* could totally derail this positive dynamic. Price controls and short-term reductions in the cost of drugs and devices would have the appearance of benefitting the consumer in the short run.

But over time, the lack of new investment and invention would only serve to work against the interests of the public. We don't need to add more obstacles to the process of bringing new products to the market. If anything, the focus should be on removing some of the constraining regulations that are now in place.

The path to getting a new medical product to market is painstakingly slow and torturous. A drug company, for example, must first protect its invention with a patent issued by the Patent and Trademark Office. It must then go to the FDA for approvals to conduct clinical tests. Test results are then reviewed by an advisory committee of outside scientists. Approval to take the product to market is then issued, called a New Drug Approval (NDA). The manufacturer must then follow NDA rules in its marketing and distribution.

How long does all of this take? On average, it takes 12 years for an experimental drug to make the trip from laboratory to market. But that's for the drugs that make it. As it is, only about 0.1% of the drugs that are involved in preclinical testing get to the human testing stage. Of these, only about one in five are ultimately approved. The approval process alone can literally cost producers tens of millions of dollars in direct costs, not to mention the diversion of time, talent, and energy that goes into the approval process. This puts up a very high hurdle for both companies and their investors.

One of the key criticisms of the FDA approval process is that it's asymmetrical. That is to say, if a product is shown to harm certain types of patients, there's a built-in bias against the product, even if it's proven to be of great benefit to others. This bias often leads to a slowdown of the approval process, even where there's demonstrable proof that a product could be safely and beneficially used by certain patient segments.

The problem is that the FDA is put in a de facto position of practicing medicine and making judgments about benefit-risk for the *average* patient. But the FDA doesn't always take into account the fact that patient needs and preferences are significantly different. Compounding the problem is the FDA's 40+ year-old rule structure and its difficulty in keeping up with advancements in medicine. The bottom line: delays and higher prices.

Frozen in Time

Regulators live in a static-state universe. That is to say that regulators have very real difficulties in understanding major changes in marketplace purchase and consumption behaviors, or in dealing with disruptive technologies or business models. The default tendency is to apply old criteria to new models and then deem the innovation to have failed if it doesn't meet those criteria. As a result, new technologies, for example, are often evaluated on the basis of absolute cost, with no consideration given to cost-benefit compared with other technologies. I can remember, for example, some pertinent ancient history with the introduction of computerized axial tomography (CT) technology in the early 1970s. Providers were routinely denied approval for this equipment based on an arbitrary formula that a CT scanner could serve a million-person population base, and that any number of machines beyond that ratio represented an unnecessary cost. CT technology is now, of course, about as ubiquitous as the standard X-ray machine.

One of the major challenges going forward will be how the regulatory framework deals with emerging technologies in such areas as digital health, telemedicine, smart devices, and over-the-counter probiotics. There's concern that the FDA and other agencies could dramatically slow down or otherwise curb progress at a time when the private sector is achieving remarkable breakthroughs.

Regulators are famous for applying rules to new concepts where the rules don't apply. A recent example of this is the experience of Northwell Health, a major New York provider system. This health system took a lead role and made major investments in implementing a built-in insurance model as part of its provider network. The premise of the model was that some of the premium dollars could be used for investing in preventive health and innovative patient care models that would ultimately improve the effectiveness and reduce the overall costs of health care delivery. You couldn't possibly script a strategy that is more in keeping with the government's stated objectives of health reform.

But Northwell's experiment failed. Not because of any intrinsic flaw in the model itself, or because of any lack of market interest. There was, in fact, a large customer base most eager to sign on for this plan. No, the problem arose from so-called *risk adjustment* regulations that forced the plan to forfeit a sizeable portion of its revenues because its customer base was *too healthy*. This is a provision that was intended to take dollars from insurance plans that have a statistical skew toward healthier customers and redistribute some of the premium dollars to plans that have sicker patients. But the situation in Northwell's case was not that its plan members were necessarily healthier, but rather, that the plan simply hadn't been in business long enough to collect and document a sufficient medical claims data base. No matter, the regulators countered. The data are the data.

Tort Reform, a Critical Need

Not many years ago our firm was engaged by a major health system in the State of Illinois to figure out ways of providing neurosurgical support for head trauma and intra-cranial surgery. The costs of malpractice insurance for neurosurgery had escalated to a level ($200,000+ per year) where neurosurgeons were no longer willing to perform these surgeries. This is not an isolated situation. On a similar basis, it has become difficult in some locales to find an Obstetrician/gynecologist (OB/GYN) who is willing to deliver babies. When you factor in the cost of malpractice coverage, along with a demanding 24/7 on-call schedule, there's a very real incentive to get out of the baby business and just stick with GYN work.

Existing medical malpractice laws, or the lack thereof, have also affected the insurance industry. Many companies have gotten out of the medical malpractice insurance business altogether. Those who are still underwriting this coverage are downsizing this portion of their business portfolio. This reduction in the number of carriers, combined with at times huge underwriting losses, has caused the price of provider premiums to soar. These are just some of the problems that speak to the need for tort reform in medicine.

Anyone harmed by medical practice should have the ability to receive compensation under the law. But state laws have in many cases supported inefficient and frivolous litigation, adding to the costs of care for everyone. The existing medical liability system leads to defensive medical practices, causing physicians to order unnecessary tests and procedures. (According to research conducted by Gallup, the cost of defensive medicine has been estimated to account for one out of every four dollars spent.)[9] Or, as in the cases cited earlier, some physicians simply refuse to perform certain high-risk (legally-speaking) procedures, or leave their practice altogether.

The Real Costs of Regulation

Health care laws and related compliance requirements have created an industry within an industry. The medical-administrative complex—our old friend, MAC—consumes trillions of dollars, and has a vested interest in maintaining a bureaucratic structure that employs huge numbers of people. There are, in fact, over a dozen professional associations focused just on health care compliance issues and related training processes. There are more pages of regulations for Medicare than are found in the Internal Revenue Service Code.

One of the main targets of the regulatory business is cost. So, how ironic it is that the regulatory industry itself, that consumes billions of dollars, has a vested self-interest in maintaining a bureaucratic structure that employs huge numbers of people. According to the most recent report by The Competitive Enterprise Institute, the cost of federal regulation compliance in the health industry in 2016 exceeded $190 billion.[10]

But the real costs of regulation can't be measured in dollars. On balance, the history of legislative and regulatory policy in the United States has not been driven by logic or objective considerations. It has instead been a function of political expediency and self-interest on the part of vested groups. As a result, we have an industry model that doesn't work very well. We have an imbalance of resource supply and demand. Costs and prices are inflated. Waste and fraud are pervasive. Consumer choice is limited. Caregivers are boxed into a one-size-fits-all treatment approach to patients with unique needs. Health plans limit the choice of features and pricing. Innovation is stymied.

But above all, we have let a political and bureaucratic structure—MAC again—evolve to a point where it doesn't really want to change the way things are. MAC not only doesn't want transformational change, but in many respects is either directly or indirectly working against some of the positive market dynamics that are underway.

References

1. A. Gupta et al., Association of the hospital readmissions reduction program implementation with readmission and mortality outcomes in heart failure, *The Journal of the American Medical Association Cardiology, The JAMA Network*, 3(1): 44–53, 2017.

2. J. C. Capretta, J. L. Chen, Macra: The health-care takeover, *The Wall Street Journal*, May 31, 2016. https://www.wsj.com/articles/macra-the-quiet-health-care-takeover-1464734029.

3. M. Frieberg et al., *Factors Affecting Physician Professional Satisfaction and Their Implications for Patient Care, Health Systems, and Health Policy*, RAND Corporation, Washington, DC, pp. 33–45, 2013.

4. L. Kane, N. Chesanow, *Medscape EHR Report 2014*, WebMD LLC, New York, pp. 18–19, July 15, 2014.

5. M. Trapani, It's time to get doctors out of EHR data entry, *Medical Economics*, June 11, 2016. http://medicaleconomics .modernmedicine.com/medical-economics/news/ its-time-get-doctors-out-ehr-data-entry.

6. J. Clemens, J. D. Gottlieb, *In the Shadow of a Giant: Medicare's Influence on Private Physician Payments*, University of California San Diego Department of Economics, UCSD and NBER UBC and NBER, San Diego, CA, August 31, 2015.

7. C. Pope, Legislating low prices: Cutting costs or care? *The Heritage Foundation*, August 9, 2013.

8. M. Olhausen, Certificate of need laws: A prescription for higher costs, *Antitrust*, Vol. 30. No. 1 (Fall 2015), American Bar Association, Chicago, IL, p. 53.

9. W. Oliver, Ending defensive medicine is the key to containing health care costs, *Investor's Business Daily Commentary*, March 24, 2017.

10. *The Ten Thousand Commandments*, The Competitive Enterprise Institute, Washington, DC, May 2017.

Chapter 7

Where's the Competition?

"Monopoly is business at the end of its journey."

—Henry DeMerest Lloyd, Journalist

CHAPTER OVERVIEW

- The overall effect of government policy has been to reduce competition.
- Independent physician practices are becoming the *Bigfoot* of modern medicine.
- The insurance industry is consolidating in response to policy direction.
- The government is sending mixed signals on the virtues of competition versus integration.
- The consumer is caught in the middle of a scorched-earth battle between providers, insurers, and the government.

Competition and Value

In simple economic terms, a competitive market is one in which buyers and sellers come together in an exchange relationship in a manner that provides the most value to all parties. There's been a long-standing argument that competition in health care is limited by the inability of the market to determine and compare value. Some have gone so far as to suggest that, because we can't really measure value in a meaningful way, that health care should be considered and regulated as a utility.

But of course, we *can* measure value in health care. We can quantify and compare provider value as determined by patient outcomes, cost of care, efficacy (costs relative to outcomes), and level of patient satisfaction. We can measure and compare insurance value in terms of costs and health benefits. These value comparisons are made all the time and, in the case of provider measures, are becoming increasingly meaningful with the availability of Big Data and comparative performance metrics.

I can personally attest to both the role and value of competition in the provider segment. My firm has been extensively involved in assisting leading health systems in the development of strategies for attaining competitive advantage through comparative value. Such strategies are focused on product (clinical distinction and centers of excellence), processes (care coordination and integration), and platform design (where and how delivery assets are geographically distributed for optimal access and efficiency). These strategies are then linked to measures of attainment that are tracked over time with the corresponding metrics for competing organizations. The bottom line is that competition provides enormous benefits to all parties: providers, purchasers, and most important, patients. It keeps organizations focused and ensures that they are being responsive to the market in providing and improving value.

Likewise, health care plans have historically had to be competitive in the marketplace. Insurance company strategists have devoted considerable time and resources in developing products that are tailored to market needs. But as discussed in the previous chapter and later in the chapter, this competitive dynamic has been largely eliminated by government's intrusion into this industry.

More Government, Less Competition

The architects of Obamacare pushed strongly toward a health care model that would, in theory at least, produce better results through the standardization and cross-provider coordination of clinical services. The law would "unleash forces that favor integration across the continuum of care," wrote Dr. Ezekiel Emanuel and two other coauthors of the Affordable Care Act (ACA).[1]

The thrust of Obamacare was one of corporatism, which is to say that there was a built-in premise that larger systems are more efficient. (There was also an implicit recognition that a market with just a few players would make it easier to control those entities and promulgate the standardization of care.) In practical effect, the requirements and incentives posed by the ACA put unprecedented pressures on health care providers to affiliate, merge, or otherwise collaborate.

There's also been a recognition that the financial resources of larger systems are necessary to take care of indigent (*self-pay*) patients and to provide needed emergency services. Medicare rates and reimbursement methodologies for hospital outpatient departments (HOPDs) have been structured in a way that gives established health care systems advantages over free-standing specialty outpatient facilities. And as discussed earlier, existing Certificate of Need (CON) laws have been successfully used by large provider systems to thwart the development or expansion of competing facilities.

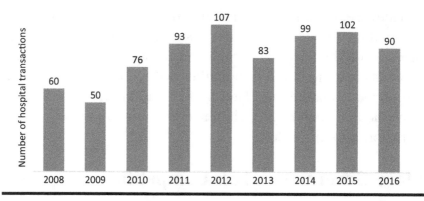

Figure 7.1   Hospital M&A Transactions (2008–2016). (From Irving Levin Associates, Norwalk, CT, 2016.)

The net result of this was predictable. There's been a decided trend for providers—both hospitals and physicians—to merge into larger systems that have come to dominate many markets. The following graph shows the dramatic increase in hospital mergers and acquisitions since the passage of the ACA in 2010 (Figure 7.1).

The timing of this upsurge in mergers hasn't been one of coincidence. I have been involved in a number of pre-merger discussions with health system executives and board members since the passage of the ACA. They have been very specific about the impact of Obamacare on their business model, and how it has led them toward looking at the options for merger and consolidation.

Another, related factor that is driving market consolidation is the shift to value- and risk-based payment. This has had a predictable impact on market structure, since there is added pressure on the part of delivery systems to expand their scale of operations, plus control more of the stages of production (Figure 7.2).

As a consequence of all of this, we've seen an acceleration in the evolution of large-scale health care delivery systems. Whereas, we used to have largely independent hospitals with medical staffs of independent physicians, we now have

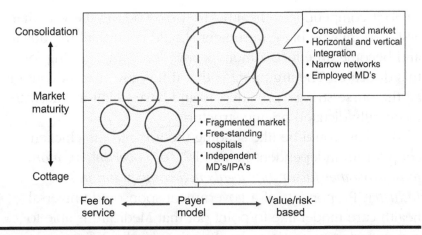

Figure 7.2   Evolving market structure.

integrated health systems that encompass multiple hospitals and physicians who are either employed or in aligned physician corporations. Today, out of a total of over 4,800 community hospitals the U.S., almost two-thirds are part of larger health care systems.[2] The typical market—even in a large metropolitan region—now has only three or four consolidated health care systems, and maybe just a few fringe players. Many markets in less populated areas have only one provider system or facility.

With fewer players in a given market, we're seeing more and more evidence of a cartel-like alliance between providers and insurers. An example that just recently got on the public radar screen involved Partners Health, a major Boston-area provider system, and Massachusetts Blue Cross. In this instance, Partners entered into an agreement with Blue Cross that essentially guaranteed that no other health insurer could pay lower rates than Blue Cross. Sadly, this form of collusion, if you want to call it that, isn't an isolated instance. It's a common practice now for insurers to negotiate *most-favored nation* clauses with provider systems. On this basis, providers charge other insurers higher rates, resulting in higher prices to the consumer.

So if competition in health care isn't working the way that it should, maybe big government should control all the dollars and become, in effect, a monopsony? Some are pushing for this direction. The argument is that if the government controls all the purse strings, providers would have to fall in line with a centrally dictated pricing structure.

But that would be like sending the fox into the chicken coop for an independent hen audit. *The government, more than any other factor, has weakened competition in the industry.* Proponents of a government-sponsored universal health care model like to point out that Medicare is able to pay providers at a pricing level that's typically 25% or so less than what is charged to private insurance. But this argument ignores the reality that Medicare prices are *administered* and not necessarily value-based, along with the fact that health systems need to extract higher prices from the private market in order to cross-subsidize Medicare.

Independent Physicians: An Endangered Species

The government has also played a significant role in physicians' desire to get out of the independent practice of medicine. Reimbursement policies make it difficult for independent practices, particularly small practices, to stay on top of administrative and compliance processes. Private health insurance companies also place growing red-tape burdens on the independent doctor.

So while hospitals have been consolidating at a fast clip, so have physician practices. If current trends continue, *the solo practitioner will soon become the rarely sighted Bigfoot of the health care professional world.* Over a 20-year period from 1983 to 2014, the proportion of physicians in solo status declined from over 40% to 17%. During this same period, the percentage of physicians in *large* practices (25+ physicians) has grown from 5% to 20%.[3]

Over 25% of physician practices were owned by health systems as of mid-year 2015. This was a 50% jump in the number of hospital-employed doctors in just a three-year period.[4] Reasons given by doctors for this trend include concerns about the overhead and costs of having their own practice, as well as a desire to put their time and attention to patient care as opposed to dealing with administrative complexities.

Perhaps even more telling, over 90% of medical residents now say that they would prefer employment with salary for their first job, as opposed to any form of independent practice income guarantee or loan. They indicate a desire for free time as their main concern, along with the burden of paying off educational debt.[5]

Eroding Competition in the Insurance Market

The merger trend that has characterized the provider segment is also rampant in the insurance market. The national market is dominated by the so-called Big Five companies: WellPoint, CIGNA, Aetna, UnitedHealthcare, and Humana. Together, they insure about one-half of the insured population in the U.S. And then there are the Blue Cross and Blue Shield-affiliated plans, which operate in all 50 states and account for slightly over 40% of the insured population.

The level of concentration within the insurance industry is a growing concern. Economists often use a *four-firm* market concentration level as a relative index of how consolidated a given industry is. When you look at the trend over recent years of the four largest insurers—Blue Cross Blue Shield (BC BS)/Anthem, UnitedHealthcare, Aetna, and Cigna—this index is now over 80%. By way of comparison, the corresponding concentration level for the airline industry—an industry well known for its oligopolistic market structure—also just over 80%.[6]

Some hold the view that the very nature of the insurance business became that of a de facto monopoly with the requirements imposed by the government and the ACA. It has become difficult—or even illegal in many instances—for insurers to differentiate themselves. The government also put price caps on operating margins, thereby interfering with the market rationality of product options, risk and reward.

Health care industry groups—including the American Hospital Association and American Medical Association—have taken the position that the insurance mega-mergers will give health plans more leverage in negotiating provider contracts. This can be the case. But not always. Health care is still largely a local business, and when it comes down to the relevant local markets, national and state market share numbers don't tell the whole story. It's also possible that the cries of insurance wolf on the part of the provider industry might be an indication that their own consolidation strategies aren't giving them as much leverage as they had expected.

Conflicting Market Signals

Here's where the irresistible force of government policy runs smack into the immovable wall of government bureaucracy. We now have a scenario where the still-operative directives of the ACA continue to move the market toward provider cooperation and integration, but where the government at the same time is actively opposing the very effect that the law was designed to produce.

A case in point is that of the proposed merger between NorthShore University Health System and Advocate Health Care, two large Chicago-area health systems. These two highly successful organizations made merger plans largely in response to the direction of the ACA. The premise was that through expanded geographic coverage and scale of operations, the combined system would be able to better serve the public with enhanced access and greater operating efficiencies. To make their position clear, they pledged to put forth an insurance product that would be 10% less costly than the next-lowest comparable product in the market.

The proposed merger was challenged by the Federal Trade Commission (FTC) on the grounds that it would significantly diminish competition in the affected markets. After a federal court ruling that sided with the FTC position, the parties dropped their plans to pursue the merger. In a joint statement, the two systems shared their frustration with the conflicted direction of the government and the position that it put them in. "We believe that blocking this merger will be a loss to consumers and further underscores the conflicting message with the objectives of the Affordable Care Act," a joint statement read. This same scenario has played out in numerous markets in multiple states.

The insurance market has also been caught up in the government policy whipsaw. A case in point is the proposed $37 billion merger between Aetna and Humana that was blocked by the U.S. Department of Justice on the basis that it would reduce competition for consumers. This is despite the merger proponents' premise that the improvements in efficiency would enable the plans to better serve the senior market through Medicare Advantage, as well as aid in their continued participation in public health insurance exchanges. Likewise, the proposed $54 billion merger between Anthem and Cigna was denied, with arguments on both sides running in the same direction as the Aetna/ Humana situation.

In the long run, it may well be in the best interest of the markets served that these mergers were blocked. The arguments for and against are highly complex, and beyond the purview of this author's analysis. But one thing is certain. Government policy in these and similar cases has been largely schizophrenic, leading to unclear market signals and confused responses.

Narrow Networks, Narrower Choices

Broadly defined, a network is a pool of providers with whom an insurance plan has contracted to serve enrollees at negotiated rates. A so-called *narrow* network is one that provides enrollees with access to a select group of providers in a given market, usually less than 70% of the total hospital market.

Insurance companies negotiate favorable rates with these networks, and in return, deliver their enrollees to these providers as patients. The premiums for narrow network plans tend to be lower than for broad networks. Which should be good for the consumer, right?

The problem is that narrow networks may be so narrowly constructed that they limit the ability of patients to obtain certain services or access them in a timely manner. Studies have shown that a number of such networks are missing one or more medical specialties. Or there may be such a limited number of providers in the network that getting access involves lengthy waiting periods. And sadly, some patients find out that a given hospital or physician is out-of-network after they have received a shocking bill. This recently happened to an acquaintance of mine, who wound up with a bill of over $30,000, having gone to an out-of-network hospital emergency department, when an in-network facility was only blocks away. He was unaware of the network relationships and exclusions, since they had recently changed.

To make matters worse, some hospitals may have a network relationship, but contracted physicians who provide emergency services or other specialized care may be out-of-network. This is incredibly confusing to the average consumer. Recognizing this problem, the State of New York has passed a law that stipulates that patients do not have to pay out-of-network charges for emergency services that are higher than in-network prices. Plans in California and certain other states now have to provide documentation that their enrollees do in fact provide enrollees with access to network providers.

Consumers Caught in the Middle

What we have is a three-way scorched-earth battle going on between provider systems, insurers, and the federal government. Provider systems and networks are aggregating in local markets to have stronger price-negotiating positions with payers. Payers are consolidating to mitigate this negotiating advantage while attempting to gain more leverage over provider costs. Government agencies are fighting all of this on the grounds that these developments are anti-competitive. But the truth is that it's the government that has managed to screw things up through policies that interfere with normal market signals and discipline. In all cases, it's the consumer who winds up caught in the middle.

So, do we have this straight? Too much market concentration and power in the hands of a few is not good. Unless, that is, all of the control is in the hands of the government. That's the argument that some seem to be making. That the very government that has created the market conditions leading toward market concentration—and the government that is fighting such concentration with vigorous anti-trust actions—is the same government that we should trust to run our entire health system?

Stay tuned for the next chapter.

References

1. E. Emanuel, The affordable care act and the future of clinical medicine: The opportunities and challenges, *Annals of Internal Medicine*, 153(8): 536–539, August 24, 2010, Chicago, IL.
2. Annual Hospital Survey, American Hospital Association, 2015.
3. C. K. Kane, D. W. Emmons, New data on physician practice arrangements, American Medical Association, 2013; Updated Data on Physician Practice Arrangements: Inching Toward Hospital Ownership, American Medical Association, Chicago, IL, 2015.

4. Based on research conducted by Physician Advisory Institute, as reported in *HealthLeaders Media News*, on-line publication, September 8, 2016. https://www.google.com/search?source=hp& ei=E1DXWtTSKOzejwSotLPwDA&q=healthleaders+media+news+ september+8+2016.

5. Summary Report Survey of Final-Year Medical Residents, Merritt Hawkins, 2015, p. 4, Irving, TX.

6. Domestic market share of leading U.S. airlines in 2017, *Statista*, on-line publication, 2018. https://www.statista.com/ statistics/250577/domestic-market-share-of-leading-us-airlines.

Chapter 8

Why Government Health Care Isn't the Answer

"When you get something for nothing, you just haven't been billed yet."

—Franklin P. Jones, Journalist, 1908–1980

CHAPTER OVERVIEW

- Obamacare laid much of the groundwork for government control of health care.
- *Medicare for all* would, in effect, be *Medicare for none.*
- A single payer system would actually *increase* costs, with stringent rationing an inevitable result.
- States haven't been able to make the case for a single-payer system.
- The performance over time of other government-run models has not been encouraging.
- Americans don't do socialism very well.

"It's the Government: They Know Best...."

Fast forward to the year 2025. The collective frustration with a lack of legislative progress led to a monumental Republican defeat in 2020, and a universal, single-payer health care model has been put into place. Maria and José's 8-year-old daughter, Guadalupe, has been diagnosed with a brain tumor. The couple has done their own research and has decided that they would like to at least consider the option of having Guadalupe's cancer treated with proton beam therapy. They learned from their investigation that this technology allows caregivers to more precisely aim the highest dose of radiation at the cancer cells and minimize the damage to healthy tissues. They're concerned about the possibility of secondary tumors being caused by conventional radiation therapy, and know that young children with brain tumors are particularly at risk for the collateral damage caused by conventional radiation treatment.

The couple share their thoughts with Guadalupe's oncologist and radiation therapist. But they are told that proton beam therapy is no longer available, that it's considered to be too expensive. "But we don't want to take any chances here," the couple protests. "We have the resources. If our insurance company won't pick up the full tab, we'll pay the difference out of our own pocket."

The physicians then share the realities of the situation. They acknowledge that proton beam therapy would have a lot of inherent advantages in treating their daughter's cancer. But, they point out, they have no choice. Even though the proton technology is sitting idly by on the institution's campus, they can no longer make use of it. In fact, they would be subject to career-threatening sanctions if they were to do so.

Maria and José then learn that the U.S. government is now calling the shots on the treatment approaches and technologies that are available to the public. They discover that a federal board of anonymous individuals now dictates what types of health care services and technologies can be used, and that regulations now preclude certain forms of proven treatment, regardless of an individual's ability and willingness to pay for such approaches. Unlike even the infamous *death panels* of the British health system, there are no provisions made for individual exceptions or waivers. No appeals are possible.

"Not to worry," Maria and José are reassured by a friend. "It's the government. They know what's best for your daughter."

Maria and José's situation is at this moment hypothetical. But the ACA legislation has set the stage for a government body that could restrict care in precisely the manner described earlier. The Independent Payment Advisory Board (IPAB), still extant as of this writing, was given sweeping powers to recommend to the Health and Human Services (HHS) Department how broad categories of treatment should be reimbursed. The Board was charged with the mandate to limit payments and restrict services, if necessary, to keep health care spending at or below the rate of medical inflation.

Unbeknownst to many, IPAB was in fact modeled after the British health care system's National Institute for Health and Care Excellence, otherwise known as NICE. (How's that for an Orwellian acronym?) Established in 1999, NICE was empowered to declare what treatments are worthwhile versus those that are a waste of public funds. The agency can make these decisions unilaterally, with no need for any justification of decisions made.

You may recall the case of Charlie Gard, the 11-month-old British toddler who was born with rare genetic disease. NICE not only refused to approve any treatments for Charlie, but effectively prevented the parents from transporting him to the U.S. and paying for the treatment themselves. Much like Maria and José in our hypothetical example, here was a situation of parents wanting to do what's best for their child. But British law explicitly allows the government to override the judgment of parents in making decisions concerning the medical treatment of their children.

In the same vein, IPAB under Obamacare was given the power to directly control the health care for millions of people. This body of people was given virtually unprecedented autonomy. Much like the highly-controversial Consumer Financial Protection Board, IPAB is not accountable to the U.S. Congress or any other official agency. The ability of this body of essentially anonymous people to influence who receives care and the types of care that are available is absolute. And absolutely frightening. One of the principal architects of the legislation, Dr. Ezekiel Emanuel, has publicly expressed reservations about the value of receiving health care services after the age of 75.[1]

Just as scary, IPAB was given the latitude to determine if a new but promising treatment might be *cost effective*. Health and Human Services could issue a *quality measure* that could block providers from offering this particular treatment. It could literally ruin providers, including private physicians, who choose to ignore these directives. In one of his speeches prior to the passage of the ACA, President Obama cited the aforementioned proton beam therapy as being too costly. Since that speech, the technology has proliferated and prices have come down. Again, this is the static-state-universe mentality of the government that we discussed earlier. Many have used the *death panel* description of the British NICE agency to refer to IPAB, also. Given IPAB's potential to have almost unlimited authority, this is not hyperbole.

The Independent Payment Advisory Board has not been activated, owing to the fact that projected Medicare expenditures have not yet hit the trigger threshold that would put it into effect. But without any overriding legislation, IPAB is still waiting in the shadows, ready to go into action.

Aside from IPAB, the U.S. government hasn't shied away from applying measures that are intended to control how health care is delivered. In the interests of "fairness," some of the restrictions concerning the availability of certain services or technologies have been extended to apply to all segments of the population, whether enrolled under the ACA or not.

Just one example of how the government has invaded the practice of medicine is the case of aortic valve replacements for Medicare patients. Approved by the FDA in 2011 as an alternative to open heart surgery, the new replacement valve has demonstrated a record of easier administration and lower risks. But concerned that this proven technology would result in more people seeking this procedure and impacting the Medicare budget, bureaucrats developed elaborate criteria for approvals that have, in effect, curtailed demand. As reported in both *Lancet* and the *New England Journal of Medicine*, studies have confirmed that these criteria were somewhat contrived with something other than the patient's best interests in mind.[2]

Medicare for None?

There remains a strong push on the part of many Democrats and even some Republicans to move to a universal, single payer system in the U.S. By the most basic definition, *single-payer* is a system where a single public or quasi-public agency bears the financial responsibility for health care, and where all the bills are paid through this system. With this model there would be universal coverage for all, regardless of age or financial status. In theory, at least, individuals would have the ability to seek care from any provider of their choosing.

The concept of such a single-payer model, otherwise referred to as *Medicare for all*, is getting a lot of press these days. This interest is being further fueled by a general public that is getting understandably frustrated with the seeming inability of Congress to make any real progress in resolving the most glaring deficiencies of our current health care model.

The arguments set forth in favor of universal health care have several key points. First, supporters say, it would provide the universal coverage that many believe is essential to true reform. Second, they argue, it could eliminate the layers of complexity and costs that exists in the private health insurance market. Proponents point out that billing and administrative costs are much higher with private insurers than with Medicare. There's also the argument that such a system would result in lower costs because of the ability of a single payer to leverage provider pricing that is more uniform and favorable to the consumer. Simplicity is also touted, as people would not have to contend with obtaining insurance, insurance networks, out-of-network billing, co-payments, and so on.

Senator Bernie Sanders from Vermont, who has become a leading spokesperson for *Universal Medicare*, has proposed a phase-in process that would begin with making Medicare available to individuals age 55 and over, and then extend it to all segments of the population over a period of four or so years. (Perhaps if we put the frogs in the crock pot and turn the heat up slowly...?)

We'll be hearing much, much more about all of the supposed advantages of a single payer system in the political discourse to come. But people need to understand one thing: *There's no such thing as Medicare for all.* At least not Medicare as we know it. As discussed in Chapter 3, the financial structure of the Medicare program is neither self-generating nor self-sustaining. A universal Medicare program would impact our national budget and tax structures in ways that the public would not find tolerable. The failed efforts to put such a program forward in one small, well-to-do state—Vermont—speaks volumes about the fiscal realities of such a program.

To the extent that Medicare works reasonably well, it's only because it is a payer—albeit a very large one—that co-exists with other payers. In ways that are largely invisible to the public, health systems and other providers actively compete with one another for books of business. As discussed in the previous chapter, this competition is a positive dynamic. It results in more attention being paid to the availability and quality of services, to access, and to the overall patient experience. Without realizing it, Medicare patients are the direct beneficiaries of this competition. We all are.

But with one payer and one set of operating guidelines, it would be a one-standard-fits-all situation. Institutions would no longer have to worry about being cutting-edge or overly concerned about the patient experience. They would have the same performance incentives as, say, the VA health care system.

Medicare patients receive the benefit of cost cross-subsidization. The current Medicare prospective payment methodology sets prices that are paid to hospitals at a level that pays for direct costs and some contribution to overhead. But this pricing structure doesn't pay at a level that can generate the operating margins necessary for ongoing capital improvements. It's the private payers who float this boat. Some years ago my firm developed an analytical model that quantifies the precise amount of private patient volume that an institution in a particular market must have, by clinical specialty, in order to offset this Medicare shortfall. This and similar models are now used by health systems throughout the industry. Without this cross-subsidization, institutions would not be able to fund depreciation and make needed investments in facilities and technology.

Physicians, likewise, are dependent on commercial payer business to offset the marginal fees that they are able to charge for Medicare and Medicaid patients. Many have restricted their clientele to private and commercial pay only. Others have consciously balanced their patient mix to ensure that they have enough commercial business to support practice economics.

As this book goes to press Senator Sanders has been on the town hall circuit sharing more of the details of his proposed Medicare for All Act. Despite its descriptor, his proposal is not *Medicare for all*. In fact, it effectively abolishes the current Medicare program, liquidating the current trust fund and putting all proceeds into a new universal trust fund. It would also eliminate any health plan, including individual and employer-sponsored plans, from providing any benefits that are covered by the universal plan. As discussed in the following sections, this would result in higher costs and inevitable rationing. Far from being Medicare for all, it would in effect be *Medicare for none.* Ironically, Mr. Sanders wants to preserve VA coverage, one of the most truly dysfunctional parts of our existing system.

Single Payer Means Higher Costs

The lack of any market-based incentive is a problem for any single-payer system. If you give consumers and health plans control over how they spend their health care dollars, they'll look for the combination of features and price that best meets their needs and expectations. If, on the other hand, someone else, namely the government, is picking up the tab, no one has any real stake in the economics. It's like the food insurance example described in Chapter 4. The design of the product then becomes a politically and bureaucratically driven process. ("I want Oreo cookie ice cream or you don't get my vote!") The results are invariably out of sync with what the market is able to pay without causing great harm to the pocketbook or invoking stringent rationing. Or most likely, both of the above.

One could make the argument that the government has been the main reason why health care costs have continued to rise at a level above the overall increase in GDP over the past half-century. The federal government has been the biggest spender in health care. Up until the passage of Medicare-Medicaid legislation in 1965, the private sector accounted for some 80% of all expenditures, either through private health insurance or out-of-pocket payments. The federal government accounted for 8% of total spending, and states, 12%.[3] Today the federal government accounts for close to 30% of total health care expenditures, with state and local governments contributing another 17%.[4]

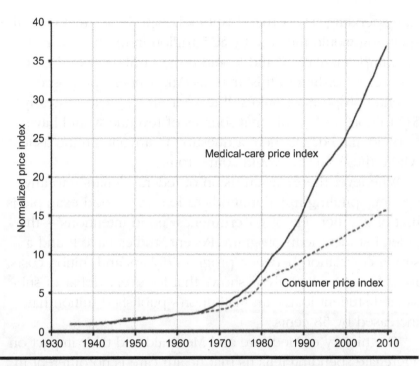

Figure 8.1 Comparisons of consumer price and medical price indices, 1930–2010. *Normalized price index* **is weighted average for a given category of goods or services. (From Mises Institute, Auburn, AL, 2017.)**

As shown graphically in Figure 8.1, the price index for medical services tracked fairly closely to the consumer price index (CPI) until the passage of Medicare-Medicaid legislation in 1965. From that point onward, the infusion of government dollars into the system has produced a level of medical inflation that is a quantum above the overall CPI.

The injection of so many public dollars into the system has had multiple, pernicious effects on the overall industry. It has not only inflated the cost of medicine, but has also resulted in regulatory structures that add more layers of cost and, at the same time, create barriers to competition.

So, back to Senator Sanders' proposal. Although the details of his Universal Medicare program have not yet been spelled out, preliminary analyses point to a major impact on health care spending. The Urban Institute has projected that federal spending would increase by $2.5 trillion in the first year of plan implementation, and would be $32 trillion over the first decade. According to this analysis, Mr. Sanders' proposed revenue proposals would still leave a funding gap of nearly $17 trillion, and "additional sources of revenue would have to be identified."[5] Is there a question in anyone's mind as to where these dollars would come from?

Whenever there's an infusion of federal dollars into any system, spiraling inflation tends to follow. A good example is that of another one of government's "good intentions"—the federal student loan program. Recent studies have found a strong correlation between program dollars and tuition costs. In fact, one such analysis shows that for every dollar of sub-sidized student loans, an institution's published tuition has increased by 58 cents.[6]

The history of Medicare and Medicaid and their impact on aggregate spending tells us that health care is no different in this respect. The default position of the government is not to improve efficiencies and cost-effectiveness, but rather, to use the crude levers of price control and rationing. IPAB is still sitting there, waiting to be called to duty.

Rationing Is an Inevitable Outcome

A universal, single payer system, however constructed, is a single control system. If all the dollars are flowing through the government spigot, it's the government that controls that flow. Because of the need to control costs, this inevitably involves various forms of rationing.

Rationing is all about control. Control of product. Control of supply. The government decides who is eligible for what services. It defines what quality is. And if the cost of benefits exceeds projections, the government either limits the supply of services or cuts payments. Or both.

The earlier passage of Obamacare and our lawmakers' apparent willingness to support a bureaucracy with vast rationing powers (IPAB) gives us a good preview of what could lie ahead in a socialized medical world. We could be facing a future where access to care is even more restricted, and certain categories of patients are placed in a queue based on their circumstances. Where wait times are routinely extensive, and limitations placed on the types of treatment and technologies that can be deployed. And where there are fewer dollars to invest in new technology, even when the benefits of such technologies have proven to be superior.

Rationing doesn't fix anything. Rather, it is itself a symptom of failure. It's a tacit admission that things are broken, and that the powers-that-be can't figure out what to do about it.

Impacts on Education, Research, and Innovation

Medical education and research are highly dependent on the private health care dollar. Both public and private academic health systems use the operating margin that's derived from commercial pay patients to directly and indirectly support undergraduate and graduate medical education, as well as research. I have been involved in many of these budgeting processes and can personally attest to the importance of the commercial payer mix in making the educational model work.

It's also critically important that educational and research institutions retain some discretion as to how and where the dollars are spent. Despite all the challenges that are presented by our health care industry model, American medicine is, without question, the most advanced in the world. Contrast this with the UK model, where considerations of *profit* override the priorities to invest in education, research, and technology.

Yes, you have read that *profit* word correctly. You see, in the British scheme of things, it's the government—NICE—that decides what treatments and technologies are worthwhile (profitable) versus wasteful. Thus, bureaucrats, not scientists or caregivers, decide how and where health care funds should be spent. There's very little latitude to experiment, or to make judgments and take risks. The government zaps the very spirit of innovation out of the equation. This is also the case in other countries where there is socialized medicine.

Administrative Costs Aren't Necessarily Lower

One of the most frequently heard arguments for a universal, single payer plan is that administrative costs would be much lower. Proponents cite such expenses as being in the 3% range for Medicare, versus 20% or so for private insurance.

But the actual differential isn't nearly as great as people think. Some, in fact, have made the case that private insurance could actually do the job more cost-efficiently if comparisons were made with certain control factors that put statistical correlations on an apples-to-apples basis.

The administrative costs of the Medicare program are shared by multiple agencies, and these numbers aren't reflected in the Medicare numbers. The IRS collects the taxes that provide the funding; the Social Security Administration handles paycheck deductions; and other agencies, including HHS, provide certain accounting and auditing support. Unlike private plans, the government doesn't have to pay state taxes on collected premiums. And while it's true that the government's scale economies might lead to more administrative efficiency, the sheer size of the government monopoly could well work against the consumer in the long run in multiple ways, including the elimination of any meaningful market competition on the basis of cost, quality, and so on.

Another often-overlooked factor is that Medicare patients can't be directly compared on a cost basis with the total pool of patients. Because they tend to be much sicker and have more extended hospital stays, their total costs are higher.

But administrative costs are pretty much the same on a per-admission basis, regardless of case severity and complexity. This makes the relevant cost denominator much higher when you make the comparisons of administrative costs as a percent of total. Some research supports the contention that—on a per-patient basis—administrative costs in the private sector are actually *lower.*[7]

Single Payer Very Popular—Until People Understand What It Is

It would seem that if the universal single-payer model is good for the country overall, then one or several state-run programs as alpha sites would be proof of that concept. But this hasn't been the case.

The ill-fated effort to implement a single-payer model in Vermont provides a good example of where this premise hasn't held up. Vermont's long-standing dalliance with a single payer model was formalized with the inauguration of a new governor, Peter Shumlin, in 2011. In a move that in retrospect could have been a bad omen for the ultimate outcome of this venture, one of the chief architects of Obamacare, MIT's Jonathan Gruber, was appointed to help with the design. At a hearing to discuss the proposed plan, Mr. Gruber was asked to respond to a former state senator comments that the proposed health care model "...will inevitably lead to coercive mandates, ballooning costs, increased taxes, bureaucratic outrages, shabby facilities, disgruntled providers, long waiting lines, lower quality care, special interest nest-feathering, and destructive wage and price controls."[8] The former senator was much criticized for his remarks, but neither Mr. Gruber nor his fellow supporters had any substantive rebuttal to the charges.

One of the key determinants of the cost of any insurance plan is its *actuarial value.* This is a calculation of the portion of a person's total care costs that is covered by insurance.

Under the Obamacare plan, the actuarial values ranged from 70% (Silver plans) to 90% (Platinum plans). The proposed Vermont plan tabbed out at 94%![9] This is what happens when you politicize the product design. In the voter's mind, someone else is going to pay for it.

After nearly four years of intense effort to come up with a viable program, Governor Shumlin finally pulled the plug. At a press conference in December 2014 he summarized the ultimate conclusion that "...the potential economic disruption and risks would be too great to small businesses, working families, and the state's economy."

The State of California is making news with newly energized discussions around a single-payer model. The current proposal would give "free care" to all with an almost unlimited list of benefits. Analysts calculate that this would result in the equivalent of a 15% payroll tax increase[10] that's on top of the current federal payroll tax greater than 15%. As of yet the overall impact of such a tax increase on employment and on the overall state economy hasn't been calculated.

Recent polling conducted by the Kaiser Family Foundation has found that a majority of Americans—about 55%— are favorably disposed toward the idea of a government model.[11] Until, that is, they learn more about what it is and how such a system would affect their lives. It's clear that at this point in time that many people don't grasp the concept that this would, in effect, be government-run health care, and that it would essentially redefine the whole care delivery system. When they understand the implications, the single payer model flips on the favorability scale from 55% in favor to 62% opposed.[11]

There's also the tax issue. Many have the mistaken notion that a universal health plan would be something that someone else would pay for. When they find out how it would impact their own pocketbook, the perception changes. In California, for example, polling found that initial support for single-payer state health care was at the 65% level. But that number fell to

42% when those in the survey were informed that it would result in $50 billion in new taxes (A low estimate, according to many analysts).[12]

Many who promote the idea of a government-run, single payer health system refer to the neighboring Canadian health system as the proof of concept. Michael Moore's 2007 movie, *Sicko*, lauded the system as a shining example of where health care should go in the U.S. And it's true that many Canadians love their system. That is, until they actually need to use it. The Fraser Institute, a Canadian think tank, recently issued a scathing report on the wait times that Canadians experience for even the most basic services. The median wait time between referral by a general practitioner and receipt of treatment by a specialist is 21.2 weeks. The average time it takes to receive a CT scan is 4.1 weeks, an MRI, 10.8 weeks. Bacchus Barua, the author of the report, underscores the fact that delayed access for Canadians results in "increased pain, suffering, and mental anguish...transforming potentially reversible illnesses or injuries into chronic, irreversible conditions, or even permanent disabilities."[13] In a previous report the Fraser Institute estimated that over 50,000 persons a year are leaving Canada for the U.S. and other countries to receive their health care. Mr. Moore didn't really get into this in his *Sicko* narrative.

In the Canadian system it's government bureaucrats, not medical practitioners, who dictate the criteria for what is "medically necessary." These criteria have not been revised since the program's inception in 1961! Decisions on health policy in Canada move at a snail's pace, and are driven more by politics than by functional practicality.

Despite its many shortcomings, *Canadian health care isn't cheap*. It turns out that Canada ranks second only to the U.S. in a cost comparison to other Organization for Economic Cooperation and Development (OECD) countries. Those who tout the claim that Canadian health care is free ignore the sizeable price tag that is buried in the average citizen's income tax bill. Plus, people have to pay out-of-pocket or find insurance coverage for basic things like prescription meds, dental care, and even ambulance services.

If we want to look at what could be described as a fully actualized universal health care model, we can also examine the UK national health care system. It makes even the Canadian system look good. It proves the case that bureaucratically run health care systems do not improve with age. *A scathing report from OECD describes a UK system that is understaffed, overwhelmed with demand, and cannot make the necessary investments to upgrade technologies and capacities.* The quality of care is rated "poor-to-mediocre," and "people are dying needlessly." The OECD report concludes that "...governance has shifted too far towards top-down regulation, which doesn't leave enough space for local innovation, and risks disempowerment and distrust amongst those providing care. Additionally, there has been a proliferation of national agencies, reviews and policies that address quality, leading to a somewhat congested and fragmented field of actors."[14]

Americans Don't Do Socialism Very Well

We look at the Canadian and British health care situations for two reasons. First, their history and performance illustrate the inherent shortcomings of government-run health care. Second, the examples underscore how people in other countries and other cultures have adjusted their expectations regarding health care. They *are* the aforementioned frogs in the crock pot, and have become inured to a level of mediocrity that most Americans simply wouldn't put up with.

A government-run, universal care model would actually give us the worst of worlds. On the one hand we would have an inefficient model that is depersonalized and declining in technological advancement and overall performance. On the other hand, we would face a ground-swell of negative sentiment that would face politicians and bureaucrats to pile ever-increasing amounts of money into a dysfunctional, failing system.

A question for all of us: why do we look to big government for the answers? Think of just about anything that the government has been involved in. It's not efficient. It's not cheap. Nor is big government especially known for innovation or problem-solving. It's not steeped in science or the clinical disciplines. It doesn't know how to treat a patient or cure disease. It knows nothing of patient anxiety and fear. It's not even a prudent buyer, since it doesn't spend its own money. In fact, as discussed previously, you could make a good argument that the government doesn't *want* real solutions. MAC is doing just fine the way things are, thank you.

References

1. E. Emanuel, Why I hope to die at 75, *The Atlantic*, October 2014.
2. S. Gottlieb, Warning: Medicare may be bad for your heart, *The Wall Street Journal*, Vol. CCXIX, April 11, 2016.
3. P. J. Feldstein, *Health Care Economics*, DELMAR, Cengage Learning, Clifton Park, NY, 2012, pp. 2, 36–51.
4. Center for Medicare and Medicaid Services, *National Health Expenditures 2016 Highlights*, Washington, DC, p. 2.
5. The sanders single payer health plan, Research Report, The Urban Institute, May 2016, Washington, DC.
6. P. Cooper, How unlimited student loans drive up tuition, *Forbes*, February 17, 2017, Jersey City, NJ. https://www.forbes.com/sites/prestoncooper2/2017/02/22/how-unlimited-student-loans-drive-up-tuition/#10003452b633.
7. Robert A. Book, *Medicare Administrative Costs Are Higher, Not Lower, Than Private Insurance*, The Heritage Foundation, June 25, 2009, Washington, DC.
8. A. Roy, Seven reasons why Vermont's single payer health plan was doomed from the start, *Forbes*, December 21, 2014, Jersey City, NJ. https://www.forbes.com/sites/theapothecary/2014/12/21/6-reasons-why-vermonts-single-payer-health-plan-was-doomed-from-the-start/#6fa37f5d4850.

9. J. E. McDonough, The demise of vermont's single-payer health plan, *New England Journal of Medicine*, Vol. 372, No. 17, April 23, 2015.
10. California single payer dreaming, Editorial, *The Wall Street Journal*, Vol. CCXX, May 26, 2017.
11. L. Hamel, B. Wu, M. Brodie, Modestly strong but malleable support for single-payer health care, The Henry J. Kaiser Family Foundation, July 5, 2017, Menlo Park, CA.
12. *Health Care: Most Oppose House Bill, Favor Single-Payer Plan— Unless It Raises Taxes*, Public Policy Institute of California, May 31, 2017, San Francisco, CA.
13. B. Barua, *Waiting Your Turn: Wait Times for Health Care in Canada*, The Fraser Institute, 2017, Vancouver, British Columbia.
14. *Reviews of Health Care Quality: United Kingdom*, 2016, OED Reviews of Heath Care, February 12, 2016, Paris, France.

Chapter 9

Market Disruptors and Transformers

"Those who disrupt their industries change consumer behavior, alter economics, and transform lives."

—Heather Simmons, Venture Capitalist

CHAPTER OVERVIEW

- Big Data, information technology, and precision medicine are transforming the health care industry.
- Telemedicine and virtual technologies are making health care very personal.
- Fusion business strategies are blurring the lines of distinction between provider, supplier, and insurance segments.
- The traditional community hospital may be an endangered species.
- The unprecedented availability of information is empowering the market with a collective consciousness, where consumers can make rational choice on the basis of comparative value.

Big Data and a New World of Precision Medicine

Several years ago a professional acquaintance invited my business partner, Mark Janack, and me to his firm's Cleveland offices nearby to "take a tour of the future." This individual's name is Steve McHale, and his firm is called Explorys. Explorys was at the time a start-up that involved the Cleveland Clinic as a principal founding partner. The visit was a real eye opener. At the time Explorys had amassed close to 50 million patient records in anonymous files. (They now have a multiple of this number.) They could access this cloud-based information to analyze and interpret a huge range of patterns in diseases, treatments, and outcomes. These data, in turn, could be used to evaluate alternative treatment approaches and their comparative effectiveness in a given patient situation. Mark and I thought we had stepped into a time machine and were indeed taking a trip into the future. It turns out that we were.

Today Explorys is part of IBM Watson, as is Phytel, which works with health systems to target population health management initiatives and to improve overall patient engagement. These data platforms are part of a rapidly developing information technology that allows patient information to be de-identified and shared, and used to develop aggregated/synthesized perspectives of demographic, health status, and clinical data.

Cloud-based, real world data are enabling health systems and caregivers to share knowledge about disease and therapies. Sophisticated analytics provide the platform for evidence-based medicine and predictive modeling. Big Data is the basis for clinical effective research (CER) and for medical decision support systems that help identify the best course of treatment and reduce errors as well as unnecessary and duplicative tests.

Big Data is now transforming the overall patient care management process. It supports patient-centered care that is not just treatment-specific, but rather, encompasses the cumulative knowledge of the individual's health indicators, history, and needs over the span of time. It provides ways for individual and patient-level health records and care processes to be recorded, tracked and analyzed on a longitudinal basis. Patient and clinical information can now be accessed in multiple care settings.

Big Data and its analytical offspring are contributing to the quantum growth of the field of *precision medicine.* Precision medicine is being largely defined by genomic science, which is based on the fact that each individual has his or her own genetic and environmental profile. These profiles are being used to identify individuals at risk for certain conditions before symptoms are evident, and to institute more targeted, proactive preventative measures. Clinicians can now use this information not only to predict susceptibility to disease, but to also predict how a patient might respond to alternative treatments and drugs.

The future state potential of Big Data and precision medicine has, quite literally, womb-to-tomb implications. We now have the ability to look at whole-genome sequencing of a fetus in the womb to get pre-natal alerts on possible conditions that will manifest themselves after birth and through the cycle of life. With CRISPR and related genomic editing technologies, we are well along the path of being able to correct genetic abnormalities before they are evident. We can use cell-based gene therapy to treat persistent cancers and other disorders at all stages of life. Even after death, we can look at DNA sequencing to help determine the cause of death. We are now able to digitize the human being in the most granular detail. All of this moves us even closer to the Holy Grail of medicine, which is *preserving health.*

Predictably, there's some push-back to this new future from established medicine. The American Medical Association, for example, has lobbied Congress vigorously to put in place provisions that would make it difficult for consumers to gain direct access to their genomic data. But there's no stopping the consumer, or the market forces that this is unleashing. We own our DNA. It's not someone else's prerogative to tell us that we can't have it, or what we can or can't do with it.

Machine learning is a key part of this evolving technology. Machine learning is essentially the use of algorithms and analytical models that enable computers to *learn* from huge quantities of data. Recently, for example, the University of Chicago School of Medicine announced that it was starting an unusual joint research project with Google to use machine-learning technology to predict medical events. Such events might include the onset of disease symptoms, the progression of a patient's condition, whether or not the individual will need to be hospitalized, and the overall course of treatment and resources needed. Google has entered into similar research relationships with Stanford Medicine and the University of California at San Francisco.

Big Data also plays a key role in driving health provider business strategies and decision-making. My own firm, for example, has developed an analytical model that enables health systems to identify, based on population and demographic factors, what the health needs and utilization patterns are going to be in a given market. This algorithm can aggregate inpatient diagnostic related groupings (DRG's) and current procedural treatment (CPT) data into relevant clinical clusters to identify prospective morbidity and health resource utilization patterns. There are many other examples of this type of analytic capability enabled by Big Data.

The Patient Is in

Going back to the early part of the twentieth century, a routine physical examination often involved the doctor coming to the patient's home. It was quite literally *bedside care.* Now the doctor's home visit is making a return. But she's not coming to your home with a black bag. Instead, the doctor's physical presence is being replaced by the applications of telemedicine and wearable technologies. The patient is becoming the center of the new health care universe.

Telemedicine is not a new technology by any means. But with the evolution of technology—including the almost universal availability of smartphones, wearable devices, and portable diagnostics—it's becoming possible to do more and more in the patient's home. Through chat bots and digital connectivity, individuals are increasingly able to access physicians and other caregivers, in many cases after office hours, to receive needed care support. Such support can include counsel regarding medications, or performance of routine tasks such as refilling prescriptions or scheduling appointments.

Many businesses, especially self-insured companies, are providing their employees with digital health stations, or kiosks, where individuals can consult with a physician via video or phone conference. The caregiver can receive real-time, on-the-spot vital signs, refill a prescription, or refer the employee to a health facility if necessary. These capabilities are not only enabling providers to accommodate patients in more convenient and timely ways, but are also starting to save costs by reducing the number of unnecessary emergency room and urgent care clinic visit.

Start-up companies are connecting the dots between patients, insurers, and providers. One example is Clover Health. Clover Health sells a Medicare Advantage product that uses real-time patient data to connect seniors to needed care services. Another start-up company called Oscar has targeted the individual insurance market of younger, tech-savvy consumers by developing a user-friendly app that quickly connects their members to doctors and other caregivers, based on their needs. It's sort of Travelocity for health care. In addition to connecting members to doctors, the company collects data from their visits and keeps track of costs and outcomes. These data are then used to refine the overall provider selection process.

Wearables are making it all very personal. Like a lot of people, you may be wearing a wristband to record the number of steps you take, and to keep track of your heart rate and sleep cycle. What started out as a device with a limited number of applications has become the technology bridge to a huge range of capabilities that will profoundly change how (and where) care is delivered. They can, for example, tell caregivers whether a home-based patient is following prescriptions, eating regularly, or even getting around the house safely.

And this is just the beginning. High-tech sensors can monitor the cardiac patient's heart rate, blood oxygen concentration, and glucose levels on a continuous basis. Soon we will have chips embedded in pills that will indicate the precise time that a patient is taking a medication. Also under development is a wearable technology capable of tracking biomarkers, which are blood-borne chemical signals that can indicate stress.

Then there's the smartphone. Since just about every consumer and caregiver has one, smartphone apps—or mobile health—provide the natural data bridge and communications link between clinicians and their patients.

A Fusion of Segments

Recent events continue to reconfirm Yogi Berra's observation that the future isn't what it used to be. Historically we put the segments of the health care industry into nice tidy buckets consisting of health providers, insurers, and drug and device manufacturers. This is no longer the case. We're now seeing a total blurring of the boundaries between these segments, and with the employer market. This fusion is creating a market where consumers have improved access to health care services, more choice when it comes to delivery options, and enhanced value in terms of cost and clinical effectiveness (Figure 9.1).

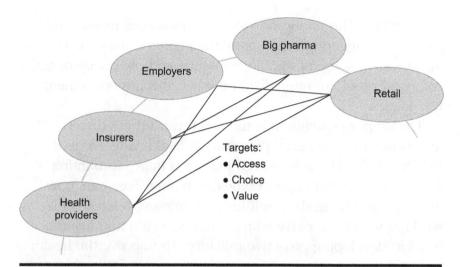

Figure 9.1   A fusion of industry segments.

Examples of how a fusion of industry segments occur are explained in the following sections.

Employers/Health Care

"The ballooning costs of healthcare act as a hungry tapeworm on the American economy." These are the words of Warren Buffett, CEO of Berkshire Hathaway, as he recently announced that his company was joining with Amazon and JPMorgan Chase to form a new non-profit company for the purpose of reducing health care costs and improving the health status of their employees. Although the specifics of how this new company will operate are still on the drawing board, the implications are huge. Together, these companies employ more than 1.1 million workers.[1] These numbers give the new operation a scale of both lives and resources to develop cutting-edge solutions to managing the health care costs of their employees. Based on early-stage discussions, it's clear that many of these solutions will involve highly personalized care delivery and a comprehensive approach to employee/provider health-wellness connectivity. The implications for the traditional market segments are staggering. Apparently the market thinks so, too, as the shares of some of the big insurance and pharmacy benefits companies took an immediate hit when this announcement was made.

The employer segment is moving toward more direct involvement in the actual provision of health care services in other ways. The self-insured market is huge, accounting for over 60% of the employee health market. For years now, medium- and large-sized self-insured employers have been working with third-party administrators (TPA's) and insurance firms in developing proactive initiatives to improve the health status of their employees. For example, many of these programs include exercise targets that are tied to incentives that effectively reduce the employee's insurance premium.

As a related development, some self-insured employers are bypassing the insurers and are contracting directly with health care systems to provide health care for their employees. A recent example is Whole Foods, which has entered into a partnership with Roseville, California-based Adventist Health. The arrangement includes a highly personalized approach to employee health, including health coaching and care navigators.

There's now a realization that the massive data sets and analytic tools that are utilized by companies such as Facebook and Google can be used to find the best values and identify inefficiency or waste in health care purchasing decisions. Start-up firms such as Collective Health are inserting themselves into this space, and are helping employers manage their costs while enabling employees to make better provider selections as patients. Taken to the next level, this type of platform could effectively replace traditional network and PPO functions.

Big Pharma/Insurance/Health Care

Recently CVS Health Corp. (CVS) announced its intention to acquire Aetna Inc. Although the thinking behind this deal was initially a head-scratcher for many, the logic began to unfold as the underlying strategies became clear. These involve synergies that could be developed between an insurer with a large number of covered lives, a major drug retailer, and CVS' PBM Caremark subsidiary, a pharmacy benefits management firm. Aetna, which has been experiencing significant losses in its Obamacare exchanges, could find a growth avenue outside of its constrained role as a highly regulated insurer. CVS has the potential to not only increase its negotiating leverage with pharmaceutical companies, but could also expand its business base of both retail pharmacy stores and MinuteClinics facilities through its connection with over 45 million Aetna enrollees.

On the heels of the CVS/Aetna announcement, UnitedHealth, through its provider services subsidiary, Optum, has let it be known that they are in the process of acquiring DaVita, Inc., one of the nation's largest physician groups. Unlike the CVS deal, which will require an extended ramp-up of physician staffing, the UnitedHealth transaction will put a large number of doctors into the delivery model from the outset.

The CVS and UnitedHealth deals are major signals for what's to come in the health care market. Both transactions are subject to Federal Trade Commission (FTC) approval. But in contrast to many of the horizontal mergers that have been blocked (e.g., Advocate/North Shore University), the very nature of this form of vertical integration is less likely to put up regulatory flags. It doesn't result in a mega-system where any one large entity can control prices in a given marketplace.

Providers/Health Plans

There are currently over 100 major health systems and hospitals that own (or jointly own) their own health plans.[2] Some of these plans are quite broad-based and are offered in both commercial and public sectors, while others are targeted to just one segment, such as Medicaid managed care.

At the same time, some health systems and their affiliated physicians are entering into direct partnerships with health plans. These relationships will be learning processes for both providers and insurers, but those that succeed will be in a position to be major factors in the financing and delivery of care in the U.S. To the extent that providers can save costs, they'll be able to pocket a portion of these savings. Insurance companies will be able to price products more competitively in the marketplace. And the consumer will benefit from improved outcomes and lower costs.

Providers/Suppliers

Hospital-owned group purchasing organizations (GPOs) have been around for many years. But now health care providers are also going up the vertical food chain to develop or acquire manufacturing and supply companies. Four large not-for-profit systems have recently announced that they will be forming a non-profit company to manufacture and market generic drugs. One of the goals is to produce those drugs where there is currently little or no market competition, and thereby have some control over the ultra-high-priced drugs where both shortages and costs have constrained usage.

Is the Community Hospital Becoming Obsolete?

I was recently on my early morning jog through a popular shopping center near my home. I took notice of several large stores that had recently closed. There was a distinct pattern. Without exception they were fairly large general department stores that had carried broad lines of merchandise. Good, well-known brands, but very little in the way of product differentiation. A lot of square footage and overhead. I'm sure that these closings reflected the availability of new options for consumers to do their shopping online for home delivery.

On that same day I saw a news release that the hospital in the community where I grew up was in financial straits and was looking to be acquired by a major health system. I reflected on the thought that this hospital was the equivalent of the general department stores that had closed: solid quality, but little in the way of true service differentiation. A large infrastructure, with high labor and overhead costs. Or perhaps another way of thinking about it is that the large inpatient care facility is much like the mainframe computer of a past era. Many of the capabilities that used to be fully dependent on centralized infrastructure can now be distributed in interconnected delivery sites.

This isn't a new trend. The number of hospital admissions peaked in 1981, and has been declining ever since. Along with this decline in admissions has been a drop in average length of stay. When you put these two factors together, the U.S. average daily inpatient census is about one-half what it was in 1946—over 70 years ago.[3]

While hospital inpatient utilization has been falling steadily, patient volumes in outpatient facilities continue on their sharp upward trajectory. Relatively complex procedures and surgeries that could previously be handled only in hospital environments can now be performed in ambulatory or home settings. The ongoing development of minimally invasive surgery techniques, along with more advanced anesthesia and pain management approaches, have paved the way for more outpatient surgeries.

Outpatient settings can actually produce better clinical and cost outcomes. A recent study conducted by Blue Cross

Blue Shield showed that patients receiving outpatient surgery spend less time in a medical facility, and recover more quickly with less pain (and cost). Spine surgeries, angioplasties, and hysterectomies, for example, have proven to have better outcomes with fewer complications when performed in outpatient facilities.[4]

We're also seeing the rapid growth of the so-called micro-hospital. Micro-hospitals are facilities capable of handling many of the cases typically handled in a community hospital, but are a scaled down to 50 beds or less, some even as small as eight or ten beds. They may be co-located with a robust platform of ancillary services, as well as attached or nearby physician offices. They're often part of larger health systems, with more complicated cases handled in the core inpatient facilities. One of the advantages of a micro-hospital, in addition to lower cost, is the personalized nature of care that they're able to provide. The comparatively small platform allows caregivers to focus on fewer patients. Patients feel like they're getting a more intimate and individualized care experience.

In many respects the market is moving faster than the traditional hospital industry in making this shift to decentralized facilities. Hospitals represent major capital outlays: Construction costs are currently running about $400 per square foot.[5] These costs are typically amortized over decades of service, so there's a strong incentive to utilize available capacities, even when overall market utilization is declining. This has led many health systems into a stage of intense competition for market share. The volumes are critical to maintaining financial stability in what is a high-fixed-cost business.

What we're seeing, then, is a market that is trending in two directions at the same time. On the one hand, we have the growth at the tertiary and quaternary levels of care that is being generated by the increasing number of patients with chronic, complex, multi-systemic problems. At the other end of the spectrum we have more distributed, accessible outpatient facilities and micro-platforms that can meet a high proportion of the basic care needs of a given community. The typical community hospital sits at the intersection of both of these trends, with declining volumes as patients are channeled to other settings.

Collective Consciousness and an Empowered Market

Perhaps the greatest impact of Big Data and all of its various information products is how it's informing and empowering the market. Until recently, the market hasn't been able to measure and compare value in health care services with any consistency. It has historically been difficult for the consumer—or the purchaser for that matter—to objectively measure and value provider performance. For private pay and commercial pay customers, providers have charged on the basis of some measure of cost plus mark-up. For government payers, providers have been told what to charge based on bureaucratically determined formulas that often bear little relationship to either the actual costs of production or the relative worth of the product. In any case, purchasers have had limited information with which to identify and compare the value of similar health care products in the marketplace.

We're now entering a new era where *value can be identified, quantified, and compared.* The market now has an increasingly rich trove of comparative cost and quality metrics that can be used to guide health care purchase and consumption decisions. It's taking much of the uncertainty and ambiguity out of health care. Patients, providers, employers, and health plans are increasingly able to access meaningful, comparative information that can guide health care decisions on the basis of efficacy and value. The veil of mystique is lifting. *We are entering an era of collective consciousness, where an informed market can make rational choices on the basis of comparative value* (Figure 9.2).

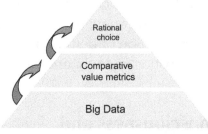

Figure 9.2   Collective consciousness and a rational market.

All of this is a quantum step forward in the evolution of a truly competitive market. In this new market ecosystem, bureaucratically administered quality and cost standards become less relevant, and ultimately, counterproductive. The traditional role of the micro-managing bureaucrat is becoming obsolete. MAC is being replaced by a market that is smarter than he is.

Consumer expectations and behaviors are also changing. We're infinitely more informed and discerning than we were just a few years ago about the treatments and technologies that are available to us. We're seeking out more patient-friendly, consumer-oriented health care services. People are looking at the satisfaction ratings for providers and treatment approaches, much in the way they're getting *Yelp* ratings for other products and services. As consumers gain more information and sophistication about their health care, traditional health systems must meet their evolving expectations. Or, like some of the old-line department stores, go by the wayside.

References

1. N. Winfield, K. Thomas, Amazon, berkshire hathaway and JPMorgan team up to disrupt health care, *The New York Times*, January 30, 2018.
2. G. Khana et al., *The Market Evolution of Provider-Led Health Plans,* McKinsey & Company Report, New York, 2016, p. 1.

3. Five statistics to know about hospital admission rates, *Becker's Hospital Review*, March 16, 2015. https://www.hfmmagazine.com/articles/1878-2016-hospital-construction-survey.
4. How consumers are saving with the shift to outpatient care, Blue Cross Blue Shield Report, February 24, 2016, Chicago, IL, pp. 3–4.
5. Health Facilities Management, 2016 Hospital Construction Survey, On-line update report, February 3, 2016. https://www.hfmmagazine.com/articles/1878-2016-hospital-construction-survey.

HEALTH CARE IN THE NEXT CURVE: A ROADMAP TO INDUSTRY TRANSFORMATION

II

Chapter 10

Destinations of the Next Curve

"A man has free choice to the extent that he is rational."

—Thomas Aquinas

CHAPTER OVERVIEW

- The key destinations of the Next Curve of health care are ACCESS, CHOICE, and VALUE.
- The roadmap to industry transformation is defined by five goals that focus on fixing the root causes of industry dysfunction:

1. Develop sustainable safety nets.
2. Restructure health insurance.
3. Change how we pay providers.
4. Remove barriers to care coordination.
5. Overhaul regulatory structures.

Access, Choice, and Value

Back to the future. It's 2025 again, the year in which José and Maria encountered serious obstacles to their daughter's care (See Chapter 8). But rather than that scenario, let's consider one in which the trajectory of health care has *not* moved toward more government control and micro-management. There's been no Obamacare redux. Instead, there has been a systematic and issue-specific range of initiatives designed to get rid of the barriers to progressive change; that is, to go after the root causes of industry dysfunction. This has led to a total restructuring of how health care is financed and paid for in 2025, a redesign of delivery systems and processes, and the revision or elimination of obsolete and counterproductive rules and regulations.

The result has been an unleashing of market forces and industry creativity, enabled and energized by the unprecedented availability of Big Data and all of its related information technologies. In our new future, health care providers, purchasers, and consumers are now able to make informed, rational decisions when it comes to products, services, delivery structures, and resource allocations. In other words, health care has started to operate much like any other market.

What does this new health care future look like? It can best be described by looking at the key destinations of ACCESS, CHOICE, and VALUE (Figure 10.1).

The following is a 30,000-foot aerial perspective of what the Next Curve can look like in an actualized state:

Access

In the Next Curve individuals and families, regardless of circumstances, have affordable access to health care. Broad-based safety nets are in place for all population segments. These safety nets include universal catastrophic coverage and guaranteed issue, including provisions for those with pre-existing conditions.

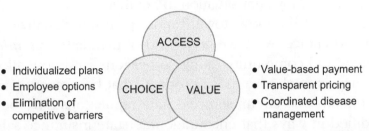

- Universal catastrophic coverage
- Guaranteed issue
- Restructured Medicare/Medicaid

ACCESS

- Individualized plans
- Employee options
- Elimination of competitive barriers

CHOICE   VALUE

- Value-based payment
- Transparent pricing
- Coordinated disease management

Figure 10.1   The destinations of the Next Curve.

We have completed a wholesale overhaul of Medicaid, making it both sustainable and accountable. Systems are in place to transition able-bodied individuals to private coverage options. CHIP funding has been made permanent.

Medicare has been restructured to ensure its fiscal sustainability as the senior population continues to grow. To accomplish this we have moved the age of eligibility upward, and at the same time have phased out taxpayer subsidies for the wealthiest beneficiaries. Consistent with the goals of patient-centered care integration, Medicare Parts A, B, and D have been combined into a unified structure.

Choice

In the Next Curve informed consumers have the ability to make rational choices among comparable options when it comes to their health insurance and health care providers. We have restored the concept of health insurance to its original intent and functionality. Individuals and families have true options for the types and levels of coverage that best meet their specific needs, benefited by the expanded availability of consumer-directed health plans and health savings accounts.

The market has been made more equitable by eliminating the tax exclusion for employer-sponsored health plans, while at the same time giving employees more options for their health coverage. Employer plans are more individualized and have been made portable so that employees can take them from one employment situation to another.

As part of the move toward more plan individualization and choice, we have gotten rid of mandated *essential benefits* and community ratings provisions, and now allow consumers to choose those products that best meet their own needs and circumstances. State regulations have been modified in ways that encourage interstate insurance sales and competition.

We have also removed the barriers to market-based pricing, including anti-steering provisions. Consumers now have the ability to make prudent choices regarding providers and care options that are based on transparent, market-based reference pricing information.

Consumers have the ability to choose the caregivers and health systems that meet their personal needs and expectations on the basis of available access, quality, and cost information. We have gotten rid of the laws that restrict competition, including Certificate of Need and so-called Certificate of Public Advantage laws. We have ended the unnecessary restrictions on retail medicine. And, at long last, military veterans now have expanded, private sector options for the delivery of their health care.

Value

In the new future of the Next Curve we have completed the transition from fee-for-service reimbursement to value-based payment methodologies. We have achieved full implementation of bundled payment and other alternative payment models. All providers on the patient care team are now operating with aligned incentives. For primary care patients, we have made the transition to patient-centered medical homes as a means of ensuring care integration and optimal resource allocations. Payment methodologies have been modified to provide incentives for high-value and virtual care services that were not previously reimbursed.

Care delivery models are structured around the whole of the patient's health and wellness needs. High-risk patients are identified at an early or even pre-symptomatic stage, with interventions designed to prevent or mitigate problems. Patient-centered disease management centers are in place as virtual platforms to align caregivers, clinical processes, technologies, and information.

Delivery infrastructures have been structured around the needs of the patient from the standpoints of access and convenience, and have been designed for efficient care delivery and transitions through the stages of treatment and recovery. Health systems have moved toward distributed delivery platforms that optimize access and operating efficiencies for routine care, while concentrating high-level services in critically scaled *centers of excellence*. Finally, we have removed the barriers to the sharing of patient and clinical information between caregivers and institutions.

A Roadmap to Industry Transformation

The earlier future-state destinations frame the priorities for what must be accomplished to achieve true industry change. But there should be no illusion that we can achieve this transformation through comprehensive, top-down legislative direction. Again, the reminder from Professor Einstein about insanity and the fallacy of repeating what hasn't worked before. We just don't have a good track record when it comes to any form of universal health care reform. Any attempt at an omnibus legislative agenda would inevitably—as it has in the past—be dominated by political agendas and vested industry interests. Needless to say, MAC would run this show.

What we instead need to do is *target and systematically fix the root causes of dysfunction.* Some will say that such changes are not possible without the heavy hand of government. But the history of deregulation in other industries tells us otherwise. Look at the impact of airlines deregulation that was referenced in an earlier chapter. Or the impact of deregulating telecommunications, which has created customer choice (including internet access), more competitive pricing, and more innovation. States that have effectively deregulated the energy market have experienced similar positive results. In all of these instances, it is the dynamic of an informed, logic-driven market—the economic human—that has brought about needed change, innovation, and discipline to these industries.

We need to unleash that same economic human in the Next Curve of health care. It's infinitely smarter and more agile than our old pal MAC, and works on behalf of the consumer, as opposed to the vested interests of industry insiders or government bureaucracies.

The framework to accomplish this—the roadmap to industry transformation—is described by the goal structure in Figure 10.2.

Figure 10.2   The Next Curve: Transformational goals.

It's important to understand that these goals are inherently interdependent. We can't meaningfully restructure the health insurance model without dealing with the safety net issue. We can't remove barriers to care coordination without fundamental changes in the way that providers are paid and incentivized. And none of this can occur unless there is a parallel process of overhauling regulatory structures at federal, state, and local levels.

In the chapters that follow, we'll be looking at the ESSENTIAL STEPS that must be accomplished to attain these goals.

Chapter 11

First, the Safety Nets

"The safety of the people shall be the highest law."

—Marcus Tullius Cicero

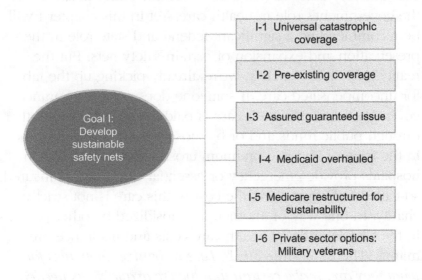

Goal I: Develop sustainable safety nets

- I-1 Universal catastrophic coverage
- I-2 Pre-existing coverage
- I-3 Assured guaranteed issue
- I-4 Medicaid overhauled
- I-5 Medicare restructured for sustainability
- I-6 Private sector options: Military veterans

Facing the Realities of Safety Net Needs

We will always have people who can't afford access to essential health care. Some are disabled and have long-term financial constraints. Others are temporarily unemployed. Still others, such as single mothers, have personal circumstances that limit their ability to find affordable health insurance, or pay for needed care for themselves and their dependents. The majority of seniors are no longer employed and, in any case, would find it prohibitively expensive to participate in the private insurance market. And then there are those who have pre-existing conditions, and who find it difficult to obtain insurance at any price. Nearly everyone, regardless of financial status, can potentially face catastrophic illness or injury that can outstrip their ability to pay or in some cases devastate them financially.

Some readers may scratch their heads or even find it a bit contradictory that I've had a lot of critical things to say about the government's role in health care. Yet in this chapter I will be recommending a significant federal and state role in the preservation and expansion of certain safety nets. But the reality is, that as a society, we're already picking up the tab for uncompensated care. If someone doesn't have insurance coverage, the cost of their care is paid for one way or another through public funds and/or by those who do have insurance in the form of invisible premium cross-subsidization. When hospitals provide emergency or essential care to an uninsured, so-called *self-pay* patient, the cost of this care is not strictly charity. In one way or another, it's subsidized by other patients in the form of inflated health care costs and insurance premiums. There's no free lunch. *Let's recognize safety nets for what they are, make certain that they're available as needed, put a price tag on them, and see that the costs are shared in a responsible and equitable way.*

The reality is that we can't effectively deal with the other problems as they relate to health insurance or even the delivery of health care until we find a sustainable safety net solution.

As will be spelled out in the next chapter, this solution is the linchpin to restructuring the private insurance market in ways that can restore the concept of insurance to its original purpose, and give consumers real choices in the private insurance market.

So how to do this? Here are the ESSENTIAL STEPS that need to be need to be undertaken:

I-1 Provide Universal Catastrophic Coverage

In Chapter 8 we looked at how and why universal, single-payer government health care will not work in the U.S. But there is nonetheless a logical and much-needed role for government in the Next Curve. It's called universal catastrophic coverage (UCC). Not to be confused with a broad-based universal plan, a universal catastrophic coverage plan would provide a safety net for individuals for top-end risk exposure at an agreed-upon dollar threshold level. And it could do this in a way that lets a true market-based insurance model work the way it should for non-catastrophic health care expenses. This is analogous to the homeowner who is covered by a reinsurance safety net for damage due to a natural disaster (e.g., earthquake), but where the owner is still responsible for basic coverage and for routine repairs and maintenance.

The UCC plan could cover all individuals except those already covered under Medicare or Medicaid. For those who have private insurance, it would take the place of the catastrophic component of their existing plan. A UCC plan would *not* replace employer or private insurance, but it could significantly reduce the cost of those plans, freeing up those dollars for other purposes, including other forms of supplemental insurance.

There are several ways of financing a UCC plan that could be considered, including a per-capita tax formula that automatically credits those below a certain income level. Regardless of funding approach, anything that we do in this regard would be, at worst, budget-neutral from a societal standpoint.

There are caveats to universal catastrophic coverage. One is that the conditions and dollar thresholds covered by UCC would have to be strictly defined by law (not by program administrators), and adhered to. There would need to be safeguards against *mission creep*, whereby coverage provisions and dollar thresholds could be stretched over time to the point where UCC would become a de facto single-payer plan. There would also need to be protections that guard against up-coding conditions in ways that game the system.

I-2 Put Invisible Reinsurance Safety Nets in Place for Those with Pre-Existing Conditions

If you're a member of a group health plan and change employers, the Health Insurance Portability and Accountability Act (HIPAA) requires that the new health plan cover any and all medical problems that you had before enrolling in that plan. That's provided that you don't have a lapse of coverage that exceeds 63 days.

The situation is different for individuals with pre-existing conditions who are seeking coverage but are not switching insurance from an old group plan or a *creditable* health plan (e.g., Medicaid). In this instance the new insurer can refuse to cover any expenses arising from pre-existing conditions for a period of 12 months. This leaves a lot of people who have a pre-existing medical condition without adequate coverage.

The challenge is how to ensure that individuals who have pre-existing conditions are not left in the lurch, while coming up with a solution that doesn't create actuarial distortions that make insurance unaffordable for others. The concept of an *invisible risk* sharing program can mitigate many of these issues.

The basic objective of an invisible risk sharing program would be to ensure that all individuals—regardless of medical status—have guaranteed access to insurance coverage. This is not a new concept. The idea of an invisible reinsurance program has been floating around for decades, and was co-opted (albeit in a compromised form) by Obamacare. Unlike a traditional high-risk pool, no one is declined coverage, and those with pre-existing conditions are able to get the same premium prices as a healthy person. The pool is *invisible* in that the high-cost enrollees are often unaware that it even exists. The pool is funded largely by participating insurers, who pay into a pool that is then distributed to insurers to cover their sickest enrollees.

A major advantage of this model is that it preserves the stability of the individual insurance market, while meeting the objective of ensuring access to affordable insurance plans with benefits that are comparable to standard plans. Another advantage is that—unlike Obamacare—people can enroll at any time and not have to wait for an enrollment period. With this model there would be no limitations on pre-existing conditions. And consistent with the consumer-directed health plan model that will be described in the next chapter, consumers can pick from a menu of benefit plans with both high- and low-deductible options.

One of the major flaws of the Obamacare version of this model was that it was *retrospective*—it reimbursed insurers for enrollees who were identified as high risk after the fact. In the model that is described here, the individuals who are considered most likely to incur a high level of costs are identified *prospectively*, and then put into the invisible pool. By going to a prospective risk basis, this model can serve to identify and influence consumer behavior that contributes to high resource consumption. And it can also overcome the insurers' reluctance to enroll those individuals that would otherwise be considered high risk.

I-3 Assure Guaranteed Issue, but with Incentives for Continuous Coverage

One of the goals of the ACA insurance mandate was to force people to obtain coverage when they are healthy, and in so doing prevent people from staying out of the insurance market until they had a medical condition or event. But this didn't work, since the fines for failing to obtain coverage were minimal when stacked up against the cost of obtaining insurance.

Going forward, we need to accept that, for various reasons, some individuals are simply not going to have health insurance. That's always been true, and will continue to be the case. Let's further accept that society, as it has done in the past, is going to pick up much or all of the costs for these individuals if they become ill or otherwise need medical care.

This problem needs to be dealt with in a way that supports the care of these individuals, but doesn't unduly distort the insurance markets or encourage people to go without coverage. Once again, the best answer is to tailor the approach to differing circumstances. Accordingly, we need to consider a multi-tier program that will do the following:

1. *Provide temporary coverage for unemployed individuals*: Through Medicaid provisions, coverage should be available for able-bodied individuals who have lost their jobs or fall below a given income threshold. This coverage should be time-limited (e.g., one year) and renewable, subject to ongoing review and future employment/income status.
2. *Guarantee issue for the healthy employed*: For healthy employed persons above a specified income level, we need to make provisions for guaranteed issue in the private market, but grant insurance plans the latitude to put a surcharge on the premium for a period of one year, and to require a high deductible—say, $10,000 for individuals and $15,000 for families.

3. *Guarantee issue for those with pre-existing conditions*: For individuals coming into the insurance market with pre-existing conditions, impose the same guaranteed issue stipulations as described earlier, and allow insurance companies to place such individuals into high-risk reinsurance safety nets.

These solutions are not perfect. But they provide a pathway for bringing the uninsured into the covered ranks. And they provide realistic financial incentives for people to maintain or acquire insurance coverage.

I-4 Overhaul Medicaid: Make It a True Safety Net for the Chronically Ill and Disabled, and a Transitional Program for the Able-Bodied

We have made the mistake of creating a more-or-less uniform approach to Medicaid coverage, when in fact the needs of Medicaid enrollees are very different. On the one hand there are the chronically ill and disabled who need sustained coverage over an indefinite period of time. At the same time, there are the able-bodied adults (and their children) who need temporary assistance but—with the right help and incentives—can be transitioned to other coverage options. Obamacare not only did not solve this problem, but made it worse by adding significant numbers of able-bodied to the program's enrollment.

Medicaid needs to be completely restructured in ways that ensure that there is some level of personal responsibility, as well as government accountability, built into the system. Specifically, we need to do the following:

1. *Get rid of the current federal cap matching system; switch to a per-person payment formula*: This would personalize the program, and give program administrators incentives for ensuring that dollars are well spent. States would have the motivation to see that unnecessary spending is minimized, since they would be able to keep any of the

matching dollars saved. This would give the state, and by extension, the individual enrollee the incentives to pursue the most effective care alternatives. It would convert what is now a cost-based system into a true value-driven model.

2. *Reform the benefits structure to ensure personal responsibility and public accountability*: The Welfare Reform Act of 1996 changed the Aid to Families and Dependent Children program from a pure entitlement program to one of discretionary spending, with personal responsibility on the part of beneficiaries and fiscal accountability on the part of program administrators. We need to do the same thing with the Medicaid program. The benefits structure, including per-person limits, needs to be tied to enrollee circumstances. The structure needs to recognize the distinctions between children, the blind and disabled, the elderly, adults who were eligible before the ACA expansion, and able-bodied adults who were made eligible under the ACA.

   Consistent with the latest federal policy guidelines, able-bodied adults should not be considered as permanent beneficiaries. The thrust of this effort should be to get able-bodied recipients healthy, employed, and off the Medicaid rolls as soon as possible. Their cases should be reviewed on a scheduled basis, with a time limitation on benefits that can be extended without re-application. Each unemployed individual's case should be coordinated closely with the Department of Labor's Unemployment Assistance programs and with related state unemployment assistance programs.

3. *Give Medicaid beneficiaries a private market option*: We need to allow state governments to develop solutions that are tailored to the needs of safety net populations. At the same time, we need to change the whole structure of the Medicaid program in a way that the remaining beneficiaries have more personal control over their health care.

This means having more choice when it comes to both insurance coverage and the actual delivery of care. One option for able-bodied recipients is to take the dollar equivalents of premium support for Medicaid benefits and apply them to available high quality private plans. This isn't a brand new concept. The state of Arkansas, for example, has received a Section 1115 demonstration waiver so that adults made eligible through the ACA expansion can enroll in private market plans. So far, results have been very encouraging. The state has seen reductions in both its number of uninsured and its uncompensated care costs.[1] Other states are considering this model.

Ultimately, the best solution may be for states—especially those without well-established Medicaid delivery networks—to combine both the traditional Medicaid and private option programs to cover all Medicaid enrollees. This would combine the purchasing power of both markets, while giving enrollees more options for care and long-term coverage continuity. The ultimate goal should be to transition families out of Medicaid and into the private market. This would allow the dollars to follow the individuals into more attractive plan options. It would also give individuals and families more control over their health plans and care delivery, while preserving the benefits of Medicaid for the most vulnerable segments of our society.

4. *Make funding for Children's Health Insurance Program permanent:* Although not officially a Medicaid program, the Children's Health Insurance Program (CHIP) has provided health care coverage for millions of children whose families don't have private health insurance, but who are not eligible for Medicaid either. This program has been highly successful, reducing the rate of uninsured among children from nearly 15% to 5% since its inception 20 years ago. The problem is that, under current law, the program has to be reauthorized

by Congress every two years. Given today's politically polarized Congress, its funding can be uncertain. The program, which has strong bipartisan support and the support of the public, is frequently used as a political bargaining chip. (No pun intended, really.) The funding for this program should be made permanent or, at the very least, extended to a longer reauthorization cycle, say, five or seven years.

I-5 Restructure Medicare to Ensure Long-Term Solvency

As it stands now, the Medicare Hospital Insurance (Part A) trust fund will be depleted by 2029.[2] The future viability of the program will increasingly depend on general revenues from the Treasury, and it's not at all clear how taxpayers will support the system.

Whereas a complete Medicare overhaul may not be politically realistic, there are certain critical things that can be done to put the program on the path to sustainability, and to fix some of the obvious deficiencies in the overall benefits structure:

1. *Extend the age of eligibility*: Under current law, individuals are eligible to receive Medicare benefits at the age of 65, with certain exceptions for younger people with disabilities. This age threshold was established in 1965, when a 65-year-old man or woman could expect to live, on average, another 12.9 years and 16.3 years, respectively. But since 1965, this average life expectancy of 65-year-old men and women has increased four years: 18.1 years for men; 20.6 years for women.[3] This increase in life expectancy will be ongoing, and will add progressively to the costs of a program that is already severely strained from a cost standpoint.

A realistic approach that has been proposed by Congressman Paul Ryan and others is to gradually ramp up the eligibility age to 67, starting in, say, 2020. (This extension of the eligibility age would be parallel to the track that Social Security full retirement benefits are now on—currently 66 and increasing to 67 in the year 2027.) Individuals who no longer have insurance through their employment would have to purchase a plan in the private market, but could receive some tax credits to help with the premiums. In this scenario most individuals who now become eligible for Medicare at 65 would be able to continue with their existing coverage or switch to another plan (e.g., spouse's plan) until they reach the new eligibility age.

2. *Phase out taxpayer subsidies for the wealthiest Medicare beneficiaries*: Starting with the Medicare Modernization Act, Congress required individuals above a certain income level ($85,000 for individuals and $170,000 for couples) to pay higher Medicare premiums. This is a step in the right direction. But going forward, we need to consider phasing out any level of subsidy for Medicare beneficiaries above a certain income threshold. Affluent seniors would still benefit from the community rating premium structure and the other benefits of a super-large group plan.

3. *Give seniors more incentives to reduce the costs of care*: Existing Medicare Supplement Plans (Medigap) provide first-dollar coverage, which leads to unnecessary utilization and costs. We need to modify Medigap coverage so that beneficiaries share at least some of the costs of care, and have incentives to be prudent in their care-seeking behavior.

4. *Promote and expand Medicare Advantage:* Medicare Advantage, which is operated by privately run plans, now accounts for over one-third of Medicare enrollment. This option was not highly supported by the previous administration and subsidies were cut. But we're now at

a juncture where the level of enrollment can and should be increased. Although Medicare Advantage plans vary in their features, they typically give beneficiaries more coverage for front-end costs and support the direction toward value-based care, and are consistent with where we need to take the program in the Next Curve. We need to renew the focus on Medicare Advantage, and increase federal subsidies in support of these plans.

5. *Consider transitioning Medicare to a defined contribution model*: Instead of the defined-benefit program that has been in place since the 1960s, a defined contribution structure would give seniors the dollar value equivalent of their accumulated Medicare benefits that they can then use to purchase a private health plan. Safety net provisions could be built into the model for those who qualify for additional government support (e.g., the unemployed or those on disability).

6. *Combine Medicare Parts A, B, and D into a unified plan structure*: The current Medicare fee-for-service reimbursement system is rooted in a previous era where physicians, hospitals, and other providers operated in a more disconnected, self-contained environment. With the shift now toward a more disease- and condition-centered delivery model, this method of reimbursement has become counterproductive. As will be discussed further in the next chapter, we need to set the stage for more of a value-based, bundled care model that effectively coordinates care between the providers and stages of care. Toward this end, it's time to end the bureaucratic distinctions between Medicare Parts A, B, and D, and move toward a unified plan with a single payment and administrative structure. This would take Medicare a quantum leap forward into today's world of integrated care delivery models. It would also make Medicare more competitive

with the private market in every way, including care- and cost-effectiveness, as well as patient-friendliness.

I-6 Give Military Veterans Choices, Too

The problems facing the Veteran's Administration health system don't always get prime time attention when we discuss the need for health industry reform. But the VA system touches an enormous number of lives in the U.S., and is an important symbol of the level of respect and support we give the people who have made so many sacrifices on our behalf.

Some basic facts: There are approximately 22 million military veterans. The Department of Veteran's Affairs operates 170 hospitals and over 1,200 outpatient clinic sites. Its total budget for discretionary medically related expenditures is expected to exceed $70 billion by 2018.[4]

Unfortunately, despite the best of intentions, we have created a huge bureaucracy that has not served our veterans well. We're all aware of the problems of the VA health system. There are the notorious patient wait times for what are sometimes life and death issues, as well as the history of a scandal-ridden administrative structure that punishes whistle-blowers and rewards tenure over competency. We can do better.

So what's the best solution for the VA system? Get rid of it. We don't need it. We have over 5,000 hospitals in the U.S., many with declining utilization and excess capacities. It makes no sense to have a separate and parallel universe of health facilities to take care of veterans, when the majority of their health care needs are similar to that of the general population.

To the extent that veterans' needs are in fact different, such as symptoms related to post-traumatic stress syndrome, affected individuals could be treated in the private sector at designated regional centers of excellence. The treatment protocols for such centers could be developed in cooperation with the Department of Veteran's Affairs.

How can we finance VA health care in the private sector? We already have a model in the form of Medicare. It could be very simple. The veteran is treated at a private institution or by a doctor that is approved by the VA. The facility or caregiver bills the government directly, with no requirement for a premium or co-pay. Or, as another model, the money currently being spent on veterans' health care could be distributed directly to the veterans themselves as vouchers that could be used in the private health care sector. In either case the veteran comes out ahead, as they would have access to nearby, high-quality community health care services. Just like the rest of us.

I'm enough of a realist to understand that this solution may not be politically realistic, at least in the short term. There are too many federal employees involved, and congressmen whose districts would be impacted economically by the demise of the VA infrastructure and the related dollar expenditures. But I believe it's time to get this option on the public radar screen. If history is any indicator, the next wave of VA health care scandals is already on the horizon.

References

1. *Evidence from the Private Option: The Arkansas Experience*, The Commonwealth Fund New York, NY, February 22, 2017.
2. J. Cubanski, T. Neuman, *The Facts on Medicare: Spending and Financing*, The Henry J. Kaiser Family Foundation, Menlo Park, CA, July 18, 2017. https://www.kff.org/medicare/issue-brief/the-facts-on-medicare-spending-and-financing.
3. *The 2017 Long-Term Budget Outlook*, Congressional Budget Office, Washington, DC, p. 8.
4. National Center for Veterans Analysis and Statistics, VHA FY16 Annual Report; Department of Veteran's Affairs, Washington, D.C., Budget in Brief, 2018 Congressional Submission.

Chapter 12

Insurance and Choice, Once Again

"Government exists to protect us from one another. Where government has gone beyond its limits is in deciding to protect us from ourselves."

—Ronald Reagan

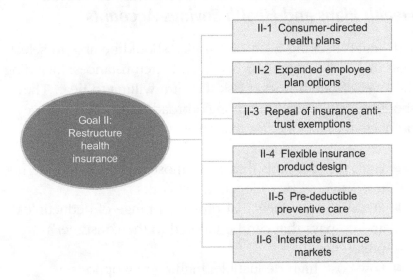

Restoring the Concept of Insurance

As discussed previously, we have redefined the role and function of health care insurance to the point where it's not really insurance anymore. Looking at the root causes of industry dysfunction, this circumstance has probably had more negative impact on the industry than any other single factor. Much of what is considered *insurance* is in reality a form of prepayment for health care, including routine, predictable services. Plan designs effectively shield consumers from the costs of care, resulting in the overuse of health resources. This has fueled the soaring prices of insurance premiums. And despite all of this, we still have a significant portion of the public who is not protected from the medical *hurricane*—the catastrophic illness or injury that can lead to bankruptcy.

We need to restore health insurance to its original intent and functionality. The following are the ESSENTIAL STEPS that must be accomplished.

II-1 Promote the Growth of Consumer-Directed Health Plans and Health Savings Accounts

Individuals seeking health insurance should be able to select a plan that best meets their needs and circumstances, including the level of out-of-pocket risk they are willing to bear. They should be able to select among a broad range of insurance products that include, for example:

- High-price options that cover most expenses and are not restrictive re: providers and networks
- Mid-range products that provide a range of deductibles and co-pays that can be tailored to the consumer's preferences
- Low-cost, high-deductible, high co-pay options

One of the most promising products is the consumer-directed health plan (CDHP). As CDHP is a high-deductible plan that requires greater out-of-pocket expenditures before the deductible kicks in. In exchange, the premiums are typically much lower. They're not for everyone, to be sure. But individuals should be able to make that decision. They can weigh the trade-offs and select this type of plan if it fits their needs. People who are not heavy users of expensive medications, for example, may find this to be a particularly good option. Another advantage is that networks are not necessarily limited, as they are with HMOs and other products.

The typical CDHP is offered in conjunction with a personal spending account—usually a health savings account (HSA). HSAs give individuals a tax-free way of putting funds aside to pay for their deductibles and other outlays. HSAs limit annual contributions, but the funds roll over at the end of the year. Health Savings Accounts were not favored by the Obama administration, and still come under fire from those who support the notion that health insurance should cover any and all expenses. But they have become increasingly popular, with over 20 million people now enrolled in HSA-qualified plans. Going forward, we need to make HSAs easier to set up and use. A one-time tax credit could be used to provide the incentive for individuals to set up an account and use it to pay for routine expenses.

There's growing evidence that individuals with HSAs are more likely to follow care recommendations and engage in wellness programs. They have an economic incentive to stay healthy. With these savings incentives, people will think twice about using non-generic drugs, for example, or going to the hospital emergency room for routine care. Some, in fact, would argue that we need to extend the concept of HSAs to Medicare recipients, also. As it now stands, individuals can no longer make pre-tax contributions to their HSAs once they're enrolled in Medicare.

II-2 Get Rid of the Employer Tax Exclusion; Give Employees Options

Employer-sponsored health plans are very popular. But they carry various hidden costs. They're not free benefits. As discussed in Chapter 3, the employer's costs are in effect passed on to employees in the form of reduced wages. And they restrict the portability of insurance if the employee decides to change jobs.

Employee health plans will doubtlessly continue to have an important role in the overall scheme of insurance in the U.S., but it's time to put them on a more level market playing field. To accomplish this, there are two specific things that we need to do.

1. *Eliminate the employer's tax exemption*: The tax exemptions are inherently unfair. They give the relatively well-off individuals who are enrolled in employer group plans a tax loophole that the rest of the population doesn't have. Further, this loophole significantly reduces tax revenues, requiring that taxpayers (all of us) make up the difference in other ways.

   Getting rid of the tax exemption is not an easy sell from a political standpoint. One approach to making such a change more palatable to existing group plan members would be to simultaneously lower tax rates to help offset the impact on taxable income. Some analysts have calculated that if we lowered marginal tax rates by, say, 3 percentage points, and reduced the payroll tax by 1%, the typical employee's effective tax rate would be much as before. This revision wasn't really on the table in the most recent 2017 revisions to the tax code, but could be included now as an addendum provision.

   Another option would be to level the playing field by providing health care tax credits to *all* individuals, regardless of their employment status. These credits would be refundable, which would put cash in the pocket of low-income individuals who owe little or no taxes.

This proposal shouldn't be presented as a negative-sum proposal for Americans who currently benefit from this tax deduction. Instead, it should be considered as an opportunity to trade the current deduction—which has many downside effects—for more insurance choices and greater portability.

2. *Give employees options for individual plans and health reimbursement accounts*: Employees who have group insurance would in many cases be better off with an individual plan that is sponsored by the company. Instead of being handcuffed by their current plan when it comes to changing employee status, an individual plan would allow them to keep that plan if they change jobs, leave to raise a family, or retire. Perhaps more important, they would have continuity in their provider network relationships if they choose to leave their employment.

Currently it's possible for employers to set up private exchanges to give employees a choice of health plans, and then make a defined contribution to an employee's *health reimbursement account* (HRA). An HRA reimburses employees for medical expenses as well as health insurance premium costs. With recent changes to federal legislation, this benefit is now available to employees of small businesses with fewer than 50 employees.

The ability of employees to use their HRA accounts to purchase insurance on the individual market is still limited, however. The hang-up comes from restrictions on using pre-tax dollars to purchase insurance that may not conform to community rating rules. The solution to this dilemma is simple: Eliminate the employer tax exemption, per the earlier. And get rid of mandatory community rating (see II-4). Let the employee purchase the type of plan that best meets her or his personal needs.

II-3 Repeal Anti-Trust Exemptions; Energize Competition in the Insurance Market

As discussed in Chapter 6, the 1945 McCarran-Ferguson Act exempts insurance companies from antitrust regulation. This legislation was initially passed to allow information sharing among small insurers so that they could set premiums at the right level. But there's no longer a need for this exemption, since the data exchange that was previously illegal is now permitted under current antitrust provisions. And as noted previously, we're now witnessing an unprecedented period of mergers and consolidations in the insurance industry, partly in response to the new market conditions posed by Obamacare. This increasingly consolidated market structure brings with it an environment that allows insurance companies to engage in anti-competitive behavior, including market allocation and collusive behavior regarding bids and pricing, and so on. In any case, the health insurance market is widely regarded as one of the least competitive in the nation. The transparency that exists in other industries is largely lacking.

As of this writing several bills to repeal the exemption have been introduced in Congress. It's time to move ahead with this legislation.

II-4 Eliminate Regulations That Standardize Insurance Product Design

A pre-condition for an efficiently functioning health insurance market is to get rid of the regulations that dictate artificial, counterproductive market structures and product designs. Consistent with the safety net provisions outlined in Chapter 11, as well as the emphasis on more consumer-directed insurance products as discussed earlier, here are the major steps that need to occur going forward:

1. *Roll back regulations that dictate "essential benefits"*: In conjunction with the development of universal catastrophic coverage, we need to eliminate the essential benefits provisions instituted under Obamacare. This provision dictates coverage for a defined set of benefits, including some that aren't necessarily related to the needs of a given individual (e.g., maternity care, alcohol treatment). The essential benefits requirement was both the conceit and the Achilles heel of Obamacare. It told people what they "needed", whether they needed it or not. There was a certain academic condescension that individuals weren't sophisticated enough to determine what benefits were *essential* in terms of their own needs. And it ended up increasing the price tag of insurance for everyone. The market didn't buy it.

2. *Eliminate mandatory community rating*: In addition to eliminating essential benefits, we need to get rid of the mandatory community-rating provision requiring individuals of the same age who reside in the same geographic region to pay the same monthly premium, regardless of medical history or personal circumstances. Again, this distorts the very concept of insurance. The long-distance runner who eats healthy foods and eschews drugs and alcohol shouldn't be required to subsidize those who choose a less healthy lifestyle. The elimination of the community-rating requirement will increase the range of affordable options, especially for younger people who have been priced out of the current market. And it will work for older segments as well.

   There's always the argument that moving to more flexible plan provisions would make insurance less affordable due to the risk of self-selection that leaves plans with sicker patients. But the counter-arguments are that: (a) this is happening anyway, with younger people avoiding insurance altogether and (b) the risk skew will have less impact on plan pricing if we're also able to move forward with implementation of universal catastrophic coverage.

3. *Revise rules to expand options for association plans*: Although not technically insurance plans, association plans have the potential to provide an attractive option for the individual and small group market. Because most such plans aren't exempt from Employee Retirement Income Security Act (ERISA) requirements, they are subject to government coverage mandates and controls on premium prices. Under the ACA, these plans were for the most part restricted from applying the *commonality of interest* criterion to qualify for ERISA exemption. The applicable rules should now be changed to expand this criterion to include, for example, a definable geographic area, a professional association, or an industry trade group. Revisions should also permit sole proprietors to qualify as both employers and employees. The lifting of benefits mandates would give the plans more flexibility to tailor affordable products to workers' needs. The provision of safety net reinsurance pools, as described in Chapter 11, would give such plans the flexibility to cover individuals who would otherwise be difficult to insure.

II-5 Revise IRS Rules to Make Preventive and Health Maintenance Care Pre-Deductible

As discussed in earlier chapters, the nature of medical risk has changed. Medical expenses used to be driven, for the most part, by contagious disease or injury. Now chronic disease is the predominant factor. It's more predictable, generally more costly, and to some extent, more controllable than acute illness or injury.

The problem is that insurance models haven't caught up to this changing risk profile. Consumers are covered for treatment, but aren't necessarily reimbursed for the types of services that could prevent or mitigate the need for medical services in the first place.

Health plan benefit designs should provide incentives for consumers to access preventive services or care interventions in a timely way. But existing IRS rules for deductibility don't support this model. Current rules permit certain preventive and health maintenance services to be included as covered items, but don't allow coverage for such services when they are provided for an existing condition. So patients with chronic illnesses such as diabetes and heart disease must pay for their check-ups, tests, and prescriptions until they hit their deductible. This can lead patients to hold back on seeking the very services that could help them manage their disease.

We need to revise the regulations in a way that consumers at least have the option to pay the extra premium costs for including certain preventive and maintenance services as pre-deductible items. Such services might include, for example, annual physicals, screening services, immunizations, routine prenatal and well-child care, and obesity weight-loss programs.

II-6 Promote Interstate Insurance "Regulatory Competition" and Sales

The popular position among free-market advocates is that we should get rid of state regulations that discourage inter-state health insurance sales. But there's a slippery slope here. If we mandate interstate insurance sales, we're implicitly taking the position that insurance would no longer be regulated at the state level. This pushes the door wide open for comprehensive federal regulation, which would have the undesirable effects of further standardizing plans and features. (See II-4, earlier).

Under Obamacare, the federal government has already become the de facto regulator in many important respects, which has had the effect of stifling rather than encouraging competition.

While we should be getting rid of counterproductive insurance regulations at the state level, we need to make sure that we don't unduly emasculate the role of the states from a regulatory standpoint. This is not only consistent with the federalist charter of the country, but is also a recognition that local regions—that is, states—must be able to tailor requirements to the needs and preferences of their constituents. Regulations that may be needed or preferred in New York may not be at all in sync with what constituents want to see in Utah.

There is nonetheless a very real opportunity for states to loosen up regulations and support the interstate reciprocity for insurance plans. Three states—Georgia, Maine, and Wyoming—already permit this. One of the keys to making this happen on a more universal basis will be getting the right information to the public so that this issue can become a pressure point for state legislators. What we want to do is to promote *regulatory competition* between states in a way that would encourage them to attract the best plans and products.

As a footnote to the interstate competition argument, it should be noted that the supposed pricing advantages of insurance in certain states are largely a function of the cost of living and the related cost of medical care in those states. Someone living in New York will not have the same available pricing structure as someone living in, say, Nebraska, regardless of whether interstate restrictions exist.

Chapter 13

From Production to Value

"Price is what you pay. Value is what you get."

—Warren Buffett

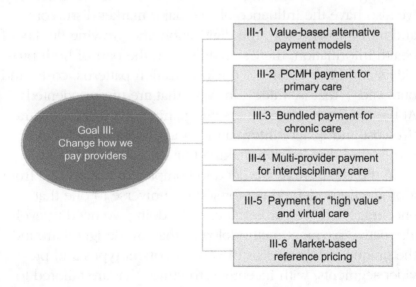

Goal III: Change how we pay providers

- III-1 Value-based alternative payment models
- III-2 PCMH payment for primary care
- III-3 Bundled payment for chronic care
- III-4 Multi-provider payment for interdisciplinary care
- III-5 Payment for "high value" and virtual care
- III-6 Market-based reference pricing

Value in the Next Curve

Under the traditional fee-for-service payment approach, we pay providers for production. And that's what we get. It's a volume-driven business. The fee-for-service payment approach has been an enduring fixture. It has literally been around as long as medicine itself.

Fee-for-service made sense in a time when most care delivery took place in the physician's office, or in an inpatient hospital unit where the patient's doctor assumed the role of attending physician and care coordinator. But the nature of patient care needs has changed, and along with it the whole approach to patient care. As discussed in earlier chapters, the predominance of medicine is no longer the treatment of acute episodes of infectious disease. Rather, it's often an extended cycle of chronic disease diagnosis, treatment, and aftercare. The family doctor is no longer at the center of the medical universe. The care process typically involves an inter-disciplinary approach that encompasses multiple caregivers, technologies, and stages of care.

Along with the shifting nature of disease and care delivery, we also have the influence of the major market disruptors and transformers. With the digitization and growing fluidity of health information, there's an ability on the part of both providers and health plans to track utilization patterns, costs, and outcomes—that is, value—in ways that are unprecedented. At the same time, consumers are gaining access to comparative cost and quality information, and are getting a lot more involved in the decision-making that affects their care.

In the Next Curve we need to complete the transition from a production-oriented fee-for-service universe to one that encourages and rewards value. In so doing we need to evolve alternative payment methodologies that are designed around the unique circumstances of various patient types and provider segments, with incentive structures that are tailored to optimize the delivery (and cost) of care.

Here are the ESSENTIAL STEPS to accomplish this.

III-1 Complete the Transition to
Value-Based Payment Methodologies

One of the stumbling blocks to efficient health markets has been the lack of relevant product definition and related measures of value. Traditionally, measures have been based on inputs—tests, procedures, inpatient days—and not on the completed *product*.

As discussed in Chapter 3, alternative payment models (APMs), especially variations of the bundled payment approach, change this whole equation. APMs provide a more meaningful definition of product, and within this definitional framework, a more objective, quantifiable way of measuring value. This, in turn, provides a relevant basis for the market to evaluate product on the basis of cost and outcomes.

As a generic model, the bundled payment approach has a number of inherent advantages. Because all the providers on the care team are operating under a single budget, they have a shared incentive to work efficiently and avoid unnecessary tests and care processes, and avoid complications. This is just the opposite of the fee-for-service approach, where caregivers are rewarded for doing more rather than less. The focus in the bundled payment model is on outcomes, rather than volume. Physicians are more prone to take a proactive role in care coordination, and work within agreed-upon care pathways.

Since bundled payments are adjusted for risk, caregivers have the incentives to treat the more difficult cases. And because they have a financial stake in the outcomes, they have built-in incentives to perform those services that will yield the best results. Specialists, for example, may have strong incentives to add primary care physicians to the care team in order to more effectively deal with patient care management, including co-morbidity complications.

Another advantage of bundled payment is the simplicity and transparency of pricing. There's one price for a procedure and all related diagnostic and treatment processes. There's no more separate invoicing for laboratory tests, radiologic exams, surgery, anesthesia, and so on. The total price is knowable beforehand. And the administrative costs for payers and providers are less, since billing processes are simplified and streamlined.

III-2 Make the Patient-Centered Medical Home the Standard for Primary Care

Fee-for-service is exactly the wrong model for primary care. For the most part it confines the doctor's focus to a patient visit, and to the performance of discrete tasks with billing codes. There's no real incentive for proactively engaging in preventive care measures, or engaging in a continuous care relationship.

We need to promote and expand upon alternative payment models that support patient- and population-centered primary care. This needs to be done in a way that recognizes the fact that there are distinctly different primary care segments—for example, healthy children versus healthy adults, adults with chronic disease, and so on—and that each segment has unique needs regarding prevention, education, and ongoing consultations.

The development of the patient-centered medical home (PCMH) model is a major step forward in this direction. In the PCMH model:

- Payers can distribute a set monthly payment to each participating physician for attributed enrollees.
- Participating providers are responsible for all primary care for this population, and share in any savings that result from improving population health, enhancing delivery efficiencies, and reducing unnecessary utilization in the form of ED visits, readmissions, etc.
- Policies and procedures can be set up related to access (extended hours, same-day appointments, etc.), prevention and health management, treatment plans

for high-risk/high-priority patients, hospital discharge
follow-ups, and clinical quality.

■ Clinical monitors can be put in place to monitor key measures in such areas as BMI, well-care visits, breast cancer
screening, blood pressure, medication management, etc.

The PCPM model is probably the most logical link between
the traditional provider organization that has a *sick-care* model
and evolving models of prevention and population health. It's
a potential vehicle for integrating not only physical care, but
also patient-oriented services involving behavioral health, dental and eye health, and nutritional counseling.

III-3 Apply Bundled Payment Approaches to Chronic Diseases and Conditions

Many see bundled payment as primarily suitable for proce-
durally related, acute care services. But bundled payment can
work very effectively for chronic conditions such as diabetes
or congestive heart failure (CHF). These models work a lot like
PCMHs, but typically require larger monthly payments from
members who have chronic conditions. The concept is that
providers have the incentives to use the treatment approaches
that are most clinically effective, and that involve the optimal
care pathways and interdisciplinary relationships with other
members of the care team. Providers aren't motivated to lean
toward those services that would typically maximize their
reimbursement at a personal level.

Some still make the argument that bundled payment is not
practical for chronic care. But we do have proof of concept.
Certain other countries are already well along on the bundled
care experience curve for chronic care. The Netherlands, for
example, has successfully implemented a bundled payment
model for type 2 diabetes care, chronic obstructive pulmonary
disease, and vascular risk management. They're now in the

early stages of implementing a similar approach for pregnancy and childbirth.[1] Taiwan has developed a bundled approach for cancer care, and now has enough experience with the model to compare the results over time with patients in a more traditional model control group. The results thus far are very promising.[2]

The application of bundled payment approaches to chronic disease is still in the early stages of evolution. The initial methodologies have tended to cover less than the full cycle of care and have focused on conditions that are well-defined and less prone to complications. But with the growing accumulation of data and experience, bundled provisions for chronic care can become more inclusive and comprehensive.

III-4 Design Multi-Provider Payment Methodologies to Support Inter-Disciplinary Care

Alternative payment models need to recognize and compensate for the roles and value contributions of the various caregivers and facilities that make up the *food chain* of services associated with a given episode of care. Such models should include bundled payment features whereby physician specialists have arrangements with primary care physicians to provide agreed-upon consultative, diagnostic, and treatment services. Bundled payments can also be used to align care between hospitals and teams of physician specialists who provide the services for a specific treatment, such as a hip replacement procedure. The payment rates can be structured in a way that considers and adjusts for the risk involved, and that provides the incentives to provide the *just-right* services.

III-5 Pay Providers for High-Value Services and for Virtual Care

The American College of Physicians defines *high value care* as "...the best possible care to patients, while simultaneously reducing unnecessary costs to the health care system." This may sound like a statement of the obvious, but many of the things that physicians can actually do for their patients to mitigate problems or potentially reduce the utilization of health care services are not reimbursed by Medicare, or by most commercial carriers. The simple task of taking a phone call from an anxious patient is an example of where a doctor can respond with an early-stage intervention or possibly head off an unnecessary Emergency Department visit or hospital readmission. But the time spent on such a phone consultation is often not reimbursable. In other instances physicians can redirect care in ways that reduce the utilization of cost-intensive services, but not receive any compensation for the value added.

Reimbursement methodologies also need to recognize and compensate caregivers for services provided via telemedicine, e-health, and other forms of virtual care. Medicare does pay for some virtual services, but subject to certain restrictions. For telemedicine to be reimbursable, for example, the patient must reside outside of a metropolitan statistical area. There are currently a number of bills before Congress to expand Medicare coverage for e-health. Medicaid reimbursement is less restrictive, and most states already offer these payments, often with no geographic constraints.

Many states have now put in place parity laws that require private payers to reimburse providers for virtual services at the same rate that's applied to in-person care. But there are still states that have *coverage parity* provisions requiring commercial payers to reimburse providers for virtual care, but at some fraction of the normal rate. Virtual care is high-value added, and should be compensated as such.

III-6 Make the Shift to Transparent, Market-Based Reference Pricing

There was a time when the price of a used car was strictly the end result of a one-on-one bargaining process between the car salesman and the customer. There were no available Kelley's or

Edmunds blue books. Oh, actually there were, but only the auto dealerships had access to these references. The buying public wasn't privy to this market information. The same was true of the housing market, where buyers and sellers had limited market information. Data bases such as Zillow have changed this.

Health care, on the other hand, is still literally in the dark ages when it comes to price availability and transparency. There's not a lot of comparison pricing for identical services within a given market or between markets. It's often a matter of blind faith on the part of payers and consumers that the price for a given medical treatment is *within bounds* of comparable services provided elsewhere.

The pricing disparities in health care are profound. For example, the Blue Cross Blue Shield Association fairly recently conducted research on cost variations in total knee replacement procedures. What they found was that the average cost was a little over $31,000 in 64 markets studied. But the cost variations were staggering. The average cost was close to $11,000 in Montgomery, Alabama, but nearly $70,000 in New York City. Huge cost variations were also found within a given market. In Dallas, Texas, for example, they found a 267% variation in cost for one specific procedure![3]

An organization called The Catalyst for Payment Reform ranks states on an objective scale for health service price transparency. In their most recent survey 43 states were given the grade of "F." Only three states—Colorado, Maine, and New Hampshire—were awarded an "A."[4] This lack of transparency has not historically been a driving issue for the consumer, who has been largely insulated from the costs of care. For the rapidly-growing number of individuals with high-deductible insurance and out-of-pocket exposure, however, having up-front price information has become hugely important. Many people now want to be able to see the price of a treatment or procedure so they will at least know how much they will be paying out-of-pocket.

We need to have the same pricing transparency in health care that we have in other markets. Health care customers—whether they are purchasers or direct consumers—should have access to market prices and pricing variations. And there should be clear-cut market signals to all producers that their prices are being compared to market reference points.

The obvious benefit of greater price transparency is that consumers can start making informed choices about which health care services to receive and where go to obtain them. This is already having an impact in situations where consumers can compare prices for "shoppable" services that are somewhat standardized. Research has been done, for example, to looking at the impact of prices on patient decisions regarding the selection of MRI services. The results clearly indicate that individuals will steer toward lower-priced providers.[5] Higher-priced providers will reduce their prices if they start taking volume hits. Increasingly, employers and insurers steer their business to lower-priced providers.

Health economists and other analysts are in agreement that significant cost containment in the health care industry cannot and will not occur without the widespread availability of provider pricing data.

References

1. J. N. Stuijs, *How Bundled Health Care Payments Are Working in the Netherlands*, Hbr.org Insight Center, Boston, MA, 2015.
2. C. Jason Wang et al., Association of a bundled payment program with cost and outcomes in full cycle breast cancer care, *JAMA Oncology*, 3(3): 327–334, 2017.
3. *A Study of Cost Variations for Knee and Hip Replacement Surgeries in the US*, Blue Cross Intelligence Data, Chicago, IL, January 21, 2015.
4. A. Ellison, 43 states earn 'F' grade for healthcare price transparency, *Becker's Hospital CFO Report*, July 28, 2016.
5. G. Sylwestrzak et al., Price transparency for MRIs increased use of less costly providers and triggered provider competition, *Health Affairs*, Vol. 33, No. 8, August 2014, pp. 1394–1396.

Chapter 14

No More Silos: Patient-Centered Care in the Next Curve

"The best teamwork comes from people who are working independently toward one goal in unison."

—James Cash Penney

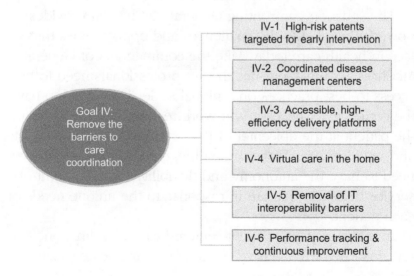

Goal IV: Remove the barriers to care coordination

IV-1 High-risk patents targeted for early intervention

IV-2 Coordinated disease management centers

IV-3 Accessible, high-efficiency delivery platforms

IV-4 Virtual care in the home

IV-5 Removal of IT interoperability barriers

IV-6 Performance tracking & continuous improvement

A Team of Teams

General Stanley McChrystal, U.S. Army, was given command of the U.S. Joint Operations Task Force in 2003. As he gained perspective about the situation on the ground, he came to the conclusion that the conventional leadership structure was failing. The enemy—in this case Al Qaeda—was operating in a highly decentralized but nonetheless interconnected network that could move flexibly, strike quickly without warning, and then disappear into the landscape. Realizing that our age-old traditional military strategies weren't working, he threw out the conventional warfare playbook and did a remake of the Task Force's authority and communications structure. He created a network that was essentially a decentralized decision-making model, but that was held together and coordinated with a transparent communications platform. He tore down the silo walls between the traditional units. Leaders were encouraged to learn from one another—to develop a *best practices* approach to how they conducted operations. As described in his well-read book, *Team of Teams*, the whole of his team became much more powerful than the sum of its individual parts.[1] He was ultimately successful in his mission to beat the Al Qaeda forces.

The situation confronting General McChrystal provides a powerful parallel to the challenges and opportunities that we face in health care today. Like the commanders of General McChrystal's units, our health care professionals need to have access to best practices on a global scale. They need to have the connectivity necessary to work real time as a team, with the patient at the epicenter of the overall process at every step and stage of care. At the same time, caregiver team members need to have the autonomy and flexibility to make point-of-service decisions that are in response to the unique needs of each patient.

In many respects, patient-centered care coordination remains one of the elusive challenges of medicine today.

The obstacles are not technological. With advanced and connected IT architectures, we have the capabilities to fuse all of the relevant clinical and patient information needed for care coordination at the point of service. No, the barriers are human. As discussed previously, they stem from the manner in which we pay providers, as well as the ongoing inertia of a silo culture that carries over from the earliest days of medicine.

As we make the turn into the Next Curve, here are the ESSENTIAL STEPS that need to be accomplished:

IV-1 Target High-Risk Patient Populations for Early-Stage Intervention

Population health has been a major initiative in the Obamacare era, and is a key goal of the Institute of Medicine's Triple Aim priorities. But it's important to remember that a population group is made up of individuals. And a small portion of these individuals—high-risk patients—accounts for a hugely disproportionate share of health resource consumption and dollars spent. The top 5% of health consumers account for about half of all health care costs, while the top 1% account for 20% of all health care dollars spent.

Since such a small percentage of patients make up the bulk of health resource consumption, doesn't it make sense to target these high-risk individuals and develop risk management programs that are structured around their needs? From a strictly business standpoint, health care systems have to take this priority seriously, especially as the market shifts from fee-for-service to bundled payment and capitation models.

High-risk, high-use patients aren't some group of mysterious, unidentified individuals. They are known. They present themselves in multiple provider situations and venues: physician offices, clinics, emergency departments, and hospital admissions. They're the frequent flyers. Atul Gawande's *hot spotters*.[2]

But there have been some barriers in effectively dealing with high-risk patients. One has to do with the fragmented nature of health care as it exists today. Caregivers often tend to focus on patients' conditions of the moment, not necessarily looking at co-morbidities (often multiple) over the span of time. Another, related barrier has to do with the nature of encounter-based data entry, the need to share and transfer patient information from one provider to another, and the lack of interoperability between information systems. This is a particular problem for patients with chronic conditions who may be seen by multiple providers and provider organizations over an extended span of time.

In response to these challenges, providers and health systems need to do the following:

1. *Utilize medical management information systems to identify and categorize high-risk patients*: With the wealth of Big Data and related analytics, care teams can now access cloud-based patient information from multiple sources to assess patient populations and analyze their morbidities, co-morbidities, and health service utilization patterns. These profiles, in turn, can be used to identify and stratify risk. An example of such a model is the Adjusted Clinical Group developed by Johns Hopkins University to predict morbidity and medical resource consumption over a period of time, based on the classification of patients into 93 categories. Other risk stratification models are also evolving in the market.

2. *Tailor care systems to the specific needs of high-risk patients*: No single case management approach is the solution. A finding that is emerging from all the risk assessments and predictive analytical models is that various patient sub-groups have widely differing profiles and case management needs. The most resource-intensive Medicare patients, for example, have a significant number of co-occurring conditions (e.g., cardiovascular risk, ischemic heart disease, congestive heart failure).

Medicaid populations are younger and consequently have less chronic disease. But they have a marked tendency to show an unusually high prevalence of mental health disorders, including depression, anxiety, and bi-polar disorders. Commercial pay populations have their own characteristics, with problems arising from injuries and neurological disorders, for example, accounting for a disproportionate share of health services utilization.

3. *Facilitate the exchange of information between health plans and provider systems*: Health plans have rich databases that can serve to identify and categorize high-risk enrollees. Providers have the ability to interact directly with these same individuals and develop preventive care plans that can significantly impact health status and the related costs of care. Plans and providers need to work together to integrate clinical and claims data, along with information linked to the social determinants of health, to obtain a shared, detailed reading on the health profiles of health plan enrollees, patients, and populations of patients. These data, in turn, can become the basis for actionable plans related to prevention and timely intervention. Clearly, there's a mutuality of interests among *all* parties—including the patient—that underscores the logic of sharing both the information and the tools that are critical to managing high-risk patient populations. This can be especially beneficial in managing the care and costs for enrollee populations with multiple chronic conditions.

IV-2 Organize and Coordinate Health Services Delivery Around the Patient

Jon Bergmann, a close friend and colleague, has gained international recognition as a pioneer of the *flipped classroom* approach to education. In Jon's model, most of the didactic teaching is done on-line, with the content tailored to the specific needs and circumstances of the student. The student can learn the relevant facts and theory on his or her own time, whether at home, at a Starbucks, or other setting. Classroom time is then devoted to discussion, the application of theory, and mentoring. The model has implemented with resoundingly positive performance results in both public and private school settings, from kindergarten through higher education, in the U.S. and globally. The approach has proven applicability across the range of subjects and disciplines. Both the Harvard Medical School and the University of Vermont School of Medicine have successfully adopted similar models.

The term *flipped* is very apt. The student, not the teacher, is at the center of the learning universe. The focus of the model is learning. It's not about campuses or classrooms.

Much like the flipped classroom model, we need to flip the health delivery system upside down, with resources structured and focused on the needs of the patient as opposed to the interests of providers and institutions. In the Next Curve we need to move to a true system model that is designed to focus on the patient's disease and condition, not just at the acute stage of intervention, but through the full cycle of treatment and recovery. In this inter-disciplinary model the caregiver team needs to operate in a seamless, coordinated way through the various stages of diagnosis, interventions, and post-treatment recovery.

Develop Coordinated Disease Management Centers

For a number of years now health systems have been developing so-called Centers of Excellence (COEs) that are designed around specific diseases or body systems (e.g., cancer, ortho-neuro). My own firm has designed and implemented variations of this model in a number of settings throughout the country.

In the Next Curve we need to continue and further expand upon the COE model in a way that provides a total wrap-around to disease management, starting with prevention/early diagnosis, and extending through the full cycle of intervention, recovery, and ongoing disease management as necessary. I refer to this more expansive model as a Coordinated Disease Management Center (CDMC).

CDMCs involve multiple caregivers and disciplines and caregivers—the quintessential team of teams—who coordinate the delivery of care with defined, agreed-upon care pathways. Operating as part of a hospital or health system, a CDMC is not necessarily department- or location-specific. It is, rather, the focal point and virtual platform for aligning caregivers, clinical pathways, technologies, and information. Care teams consist of the physician specialists and sub-specialists who are critical to providing the full range of treatment capabilities necessary for a given type of patient. Depending on needs, the team can also include advanced nurse practitioners, therapists, social workers, nutritionists, behavioral specialists, and others as necessary (Figure 14.1).

The utility of the CDMC is being enhanced by the rapid development of information platforms that can provide secure, real-time messaging between physicians and other caregiver staff. Such platforms can provide instant communication of referring physician information, time-sensitive messages (e.g., STEMI alerts), lab results, consultations, and so on.

The overarching goal of the CDMC is to provide patients with the *just-right* services—services that are the most

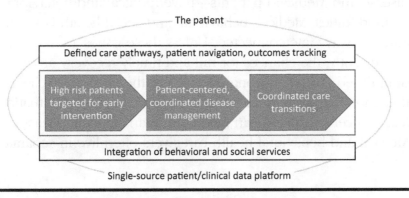

Figure 14.1   Coordinated disease management in the Next Curve.

clinically effective and that are delivered in the right place at the right time. For highly specialized care, services need to be aggregated in designated disease- or condition-specific centers, where there is a critical mass of expertise and service volumes. In many cases CDMC's can benefit from linkages with high-level tertiary and academic centers in order to tap into their expertise, and to participate in clinical trials where appropriate. A critical success feature of this model is the across-the-board sharing of patient and clinical information, and measures of performance that are applied at a case level.

The glue that ultimately binds the caregivers and processes together in a CDMC goes back to the implementation of alternative payment models described in the previous chapter. There must be built-in incentives for all involved caregivers and facilities to transition the patient through all stages of care in the most cost- and clinically-effective manner. Everyone benefits from this teamwork, most of all, the patient.

Integrate Behavioral and Social Services into the Coordinated Disease Management Center Model

It's critically important to integrate medical, behavioral, social services as part of the overall CDMC model. A high percentage of high-risk patients—particularly patients with chronic disease and Medicaid patients—have medical and behavioral co-morbidities. Medical, behavioral, and social health issues are almost always interconnected. Unless these issues are addressed concurrently, the chances for full and timely recovery are greatly diminished. There is strong evidence to the effect that relieving the emotional distress and anxiety in a given patient's situation (e.g., cancer treatment) can help them manage their disease. Medical and behavioral health caregivers often live in separate professional and cultural worlds, even on the same campus. They, too, need to be on that same team of teams.

Align Addiction Treatment with Medical Care

The good news is that health plans—both public and private—have been expanding their coverage for the treatment of conditions related to alcoholism and substance abuse. But the bad news is that much of substance abuse treatment is still segregated from the mainstream of medical care. This is despite a growing body of research and actual experience that underscores the value of aligning and integrating these two systems of care. There are also substantial links between chronic pain management and the overuse of opioid analgesics.

Consistent with the objectives of early-stage intervention discussed earlier, there's a need to bring addiction intervention into the primary care setting, where screening and early-stage problem identification can result in early-stage treatment. Addictions clearly have a direct link to many medial problems, such as liver disease, and to a patient's adherence to medical treatment regimens, including use of prescribed medications. With appropriate additional training and linkage to an addictions treatment program, there's no reason (other than outdated regulatory barriers) why physicians shouldn't be allowed to administer methadone or alternatives such as buprenorphine in their office.

Often overlooked is the connection of addictions treatment to genomic science and precision medicine. There's been a quiet but potentially far-reaching evolution in the study of the neurobiology of addiction. We're gaining a far greater understanding of the genetic linkages to addictions and changes in brain physiology due to addiction. All of this underscores the need for convergence of traditional medicine and behavioral approaches to addictions treatment.

Develop Specialized Acute Care Units for Elderly Patients

As the elderly patient population continues to grow in numbers and as a proportion of the overall hospital inpatient census (now nearing 45%), it's becoming increasingly evident that the typical acute care unit isn't necessarily geared to the needs of this segment. This patient population tends to have more comorbidities, and patients often have disabilities or cognitive impairment that accompany the primary reason for their admission. While in the hospital, they can experience functional decline, as well as confusion, delirium, lack of adequate nutrition, and other factors that can slow down the recovery process or in many instances lead to adverse events.

The Coordinated Disease Management Center model can provide a solid platform for coordinating the care of the elderly in a hospital setting. But because the needs of the elderly are somewhat specialized, there's a need in many situations to develop specialized units—called Acute Care for Elders, or ACE units—that are designed specifically around the needs of this patient population. ACE units can be set up to identify and manage geriatric-related complexities, which may be both behavioral and environmental. Patient rooms and public access areas can be designed with functional impairments in mind. Congregate facilities can be set up for patient and patient-family social interaction. In addition to the typical CDMC staffing, the ACE team can be complemented with geriatricians, social workers, rehabilitation therapists, and other caregivers specialized in dealing with the needs of the elderly.

Manage Post-Acute Care Transitions and Processes

In the CDMC model, acute-stage intervention is just one step in an overall care process. The transition and coordination of care through the full cycle of post-acute care and recovery are critical to both managing the costs of care and to restoring the patient to a level of full recovery or sustainable health. Problems arise when the groundwork is not properly laid to handle care transitions, and when patients are not given the instructions they need to manage their care after being discharged from an acute care setting. Giving patients the right support at the right time can go a long way toward both improving outcomes as well as patient satisfaction, not to mention reducing the impact on the overall cost of care over the full case cycle. This is becoming an important part of the economic equation as we move further toward bundled payment and other value-based reimbursement formulas.

There needs to be a dedicated team to handle the post-acute care processes. Clear-cut coordination responsibilities need to be established up front, with protocols established as to when and to whom those responsibilities should be transferred to as the patient progresses through the care cycle. Care coordination agreements should clarify roles and role relationships between providers in the continuum—primary care physicians, hospitals, specialists, therapists, and so on. They should also establish protocols for information to be shared and with whom, and for communications between providers. A lack of timely information can result in unnecessary visits or tests, or critical parts of the care process not being attended to and dropping between the cracks.

Another barrier to effective care coordination for chronic/high-risk patients is that traditional caregivers, primary care physicians in particular, are often stretched too thin to devote the time necessary for post-acute care coordination. But many patients—particularly the elderly—encounter ongoing, sometimes unexpected, circumstances that left unattended can result in complications and potential readmission. This underscores the need for defined structures, processes, and responsibilities.

One approach that some health systems are using is to deploy a relatively new type of caregiver called the *extensivist*. Extensivists are specially trained primary care physicians, advanced practice registered nurses, case managers, social workers, and others who provide wrap-around care coordination for patients with complex case management needs. This care coordination extends beyond the hospital setting to encompass post-acute skilled nursing, rehabilitation, and ongoing home-based care. The impact of this type of approach can be quite significant in terms of care efficiencies and costs. One analyst has estimated that the full implementation of this model could reduce the *national* health care bill by as much as 6%![3] This may seem like a far-fetched number, but not so much when you factor in the enormous portion of total costs that are accounted for by post-acute care, complications, readmissions, and so on.

Many convalescent patients require basic logistical support mechanisms to assist in ongoing care. Chronic care patients are often hampered in their recovery and disease management processes by a lack of transportation or assistance in the home. I'm reminded of a story shared with me by a physician colleague about an elderly patient who called 911. His emergency? He had stumbled while carrying a pizza and it wound up upside down on his bed. He couldn't deal with the mess, so he called 911! "Sadly, this is not an unusual occurrence," the doctor told me. "Things like this happen all the time." Simple, low-tech solutions such as providing non-emergency transportation or home aide services can play a major role in improving access to needed services.

IV-3 Rationalize Delivery Platforms for Optimal Access, Effectiveness, and Efficiency

The term *platform* is used to describe a health delivery system in terms of what services are provided by type and level, and where they are located. With the optimal delivery platform design, the patient is receiving the right services at the right time in the right place. Resources are designed for maximum clinical effectiveness and efficiency, with distributed access points for intake and basic services, and clustered high-level services where it's important to have scale expertise and efficiencies.

The problem today is that most health care systems have legacy platforms that are a carryover from the time when acute inpatient care was the predominant delivery model. But as previously discussed, the hospital average daily census and inpatient occupancy levels have been in a free-fall for decades. Leading health care systems have made tremendous strides in advancing their delivery platforms to keep up with evolving technologies and consumer preferences. But many institutions, burdened with legacy infrastructures and ongoing debt service costs, have been slow to make the needed changes.

In the Next Curve, health care systems will need to take a *zero-based* approach to the redesign of their delivery platforms. This can be done by developing a conceptual future state design that is not bound by the constraints of the current state platform, and that can be used as a template for getting to the desired platform in a phased, step-wise fashion. In any case, the health system delivery platform in the Next Curve will need to follow these basic design principles:

■ *Access:* Health systems need to continue the transition from the traditional campus-centric model to a platform with geographically-distributed access for basic walk-in care/screening, primary care, outpatient surgery; and even fairly sophisticated laboratory and X-ray services. High-tech medical malls and *mini-hospitals* can deliver most of the services that are currently provided in a centralized campus setting.
■ *Service differentiation:* Unlike the *department store* model of the general hospital of the past, inpatient facilities need to be transitioned from general acute care units to highly specialized *boutique* clinical centers, with a disease- and condition-specific focus along the lines of the CDMCs as described earlier.

■ *Scale and efficiencies:* Health care is a high-fixed cost business. Unused or underutilized capacities need to be phased out or repurposed. High-level tertiary services need to be aggregated, not only to achieve scale economies, but to ensure that the patient numbers support the critical mass of medical expertise and highly specialized technologies that are necessary.

■ *Care coordination:* Consistent with the direction described in this chapter, health systems need to evolve as true systems. This will require caregiver alignment on care pathways, coordinated care transitions, and the availability and interoperability of patient and clinical information.

IV-4 Make the Home the New Health Care Center

"In my view, the future of the hospital is in the home." This statement was recently made at a health conference by Bernard Tyson, the chairman and CEO of Kaiser-Permanente (KP).[4] What makes Dr. Tyson's comments especially poignant is the fact that the meeting took place in Nashville, Tennessee—headquarters of some of the largest proprietary hospital chains—and that one of the conference moderators was Dr. Bill Frist, CEO of Hospital Corporation of America. He was basically telling the hometown audience that their business model could soon be a thing of the past.

Dr. Tyson has put his money where his mouth is. His organization invests 25% of its $3.8 billion annual capital budget in information technology, with a sizeable chunk of this going toward patient-focused applications that support virtual care interface. Patients who access their KP app to seek counseling or schedule an appointment are given a choice between an office visit and a virtual visit. Of the 100+ million primary care patient encounters recorded by KP in 2016, over half were done virtually.[4]

We can in fact replace much of what has always been done in a clinical setting with virtual health care capabilities. Technologies such as smartphones and tablets have given patients an unprecedented ability to manage much of their health care on their own. Patients can interact with their caregivers through e-mail and teleconference. Special apps permit the patient's doctor to hear heartbeats and monitor lung function. Patients can self-administer home pregnancy tests and electrocardiograms. Wearable devices can continuously monitor vital signs and alert users to problems even before symptoms appear. An a-fib message can get the individual to a health facility in time to avert a stroke. Or a normal ECG reading can quell anxiety and avoid an unnecessary emergency department visit. Some wearables are even designed to perform certain tasks, such as administering insulin.

Access to artificial intelligence (AI) platforms can provide ongoing monitoring of an individual's health status, sending out reminders to take medications, see providers, or take other actions. Behavioral and substance abuse patients can link to AI centers to access self-management information and alerts.

All of this is will radically transform how health care is accessed and delivered. In many respects it parallels what has happened to the public transportation business with the introduction of Uber and Lyft and the connected AI platforms that have effectively cut out the middle-men and minimized the need for overhead. Extrapolate the Kaiser-Permanente example. What if the general population was able to reduce health facility visits to the tune of 50+ %? The implications for staffing and facility infrastructure are staggering.

How will the trend toward virtual care affect the patient-provider relationship? The initial thought might be that this will further distance the individual from his or her physician, and that both patient and provider will lose that direct, personal connection.

But actual experience doesn't bear this out. Most patients deal with multiple providers. An e-health connectivity makes it easier to access and interact with various caregivers, and connect with providers while traveling or away from home base. Physicians, on the other hand, have a certain component of time that is freed up from seeing patients for strictly routine, recurring, and non-emergent issues. A lot of non-critical tasks are taken care of between visits, information is shared, and patient questions answered. This time and energy can then be utilized to focus on more complex problems. Again, there's a strong parallel to the flipped classroom model referenced earlier, and the value gains that are shared by all parties.

IV-5 Remove the Barriers to IT Interoperability

The coordination of care at the patient level is ultimately dependent upon the unencumbered flow of information among caregivers and related parties at all levels and stages of care. But as noted previously, and despite the goals of MACRA (Medicare Access and CHIP Reauthorization Act of 2015) and related initiatives, there are still significant barriers to the sharing of information between providers and agencies. These barriers include data blocking, where electronic health record (EHR) vendors put up roadblocks to sharing information between organizations; a lack of consistent data input standards that make it difficult for systems to talk to each other; and the frequent lack of timely or real-time access to patient information, which can lead to missed diagnoses or sub-optimal treatment interventions.

There's no simple, one-shot solution to the interoperability problem, and the scope of issues and possible solutions go well beyond the dimensions of this book. Suffice it to say that, in the months and years ahead, it will be essential for health care executives, caregivers, and involved agencies to get past these barriers. This will involve the adoption of consistent standards, overcoming the proprietary and cultural barriers to sharing data, and the development of shared platforms that bring together the information needed by different providers at the various stages and levels of care.

Much of this can be enabled using cloud-based platforms that can support Coordinated Disease Management Centers within the same health care system, as well as tie together multiple providers and agencies in disparate organizations. The expanded use of Application Programming Interfaces (APIs) can go a long way toward connecting providers, technologies, and consumers in the Next Curve. At the same time, evolving block-chain technology can be used to provide a secure way of recording and sharing patient records across a network of caregivers.

IV-6 Track the Measures That Matter

One of the lessons I learned while serving in the U.S. Army Medical Services Corps is that people do what is measured. Most measures of provider performance in the U.S. do just that: They measure what is done. But the *what* is most often based on compliance with certain practice guidelines, largely determined by bureaucrats who are several steps removed from the actual delivery of care. The Healthcare Effectiveness Data and Information Set (HEDIS) scores, for example, are almost all *process* measures. There's an implicit assumption that the processes so measured are the right things to look at because they are presumed to be the determinants of outcomes. But they aren't necessarily *measures* of the actual outcomes.

Most providers, and for that matter, insurers, don't keep track of costs and outcomes on a patient-by-patient basis except for some very high-level measures such as mortality. Costs are not typically tracked on a longitudinal basis through the care cycle for a given patient. Instead, they are measured on a specialty-specific or departmental basis, and are mainly tracked from a billing system standpoint. And costs don't always reflect the actual expenses of labor and overhead, but rather, many be based purely on charges.

We need to look at resource consumption, related costs, and outcomes over the full continuum of care for a given patient and condition. It's also critical that we measure and report on the outcomes that matter to patients. Those outcomes not only look at gross measures such as cost or mortality, but also provide indicators of a patient's functional status after a given treatment.

References

1. General Stanley McChrystal, *Team of Teams: New Rules of Engagement for a Complex World*, Penguin Publishing Group, London, UK, 2015.
2. A. Gawande, The hot spotters: Can we lower medical costs by giving the neediest patients better care? *The New Yorker*, January 24, 2011. https://www.newyorker.com/magazine/2011/01/24/the-hot-spotters.
3. The Extensivist model, *MediaHealth Leaders*, September 15, 2016. http://www.healthleadersmedia.com/physician-leaders/extensivist-model.
4. *Kaiser's Bernard Tyson Looks toward the Future of Care*, H&HN Hospitals & Health Networks, April 17, 2017. https://www.hhnmag.com/articles/8259-kaisers-bernard-tyson-looks-toward-the-future-of-care.

Chapter 15

Less Regulation, Better Health Care

"Government exists to protect us from one another. Where government has gone beyond its limits is in deciding to protect us from ourselves."

—Ronald Reagan

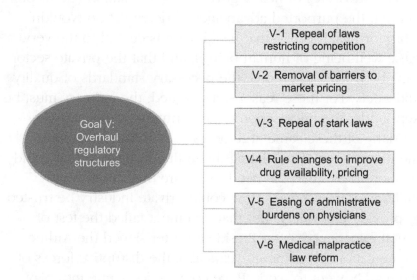

Goal V: Overhaul regulatory structures

V-1 Repeal of laws restricting competition

V-2 Removal of barriers to market pricing

V-3 Repeal of stark laws

V-4 Rule changes to improve drug availability, pricing

V-5 Easing of administrative burdens on physicians

V-6 Medical malpractice law reform

Putting the Economic Human to Work

In the Appendix to this book, "How We Got Here: A Brief History of Health Care in the U.S.," you can get a quick overview of the major legislative and regulatory events that have shaped the health care industry model of today. Many of these laws and provisions were put in place with the best of intentions. Others were more cynically engineered to advance the interests of certain industry segments. In any case, the net result of this history is an industry model that doesn't work very well.

Past efforts to "reform" health care have failed. The reasons for this failure follow a consistent pattern. The focus has been mostly on the financing and insurance part of the equation. At the same time, there's been an obsession with production inputs (and controlling the costs thereof), rather than looking at health care from a systematic, results-oriented perspective. We have a bureaucratic and regulatory structure—MAC, again that has not only failed to fix the root problems, but has contributed materially to the cost, complexity, and dysfunctionality of the industry.

The advocates of heavy government regulation like to point out that the purported advantages of deregulation wouldn't work for health care—that health care is central to the very basic well-being of human beings, and that the private sector can't be trusted to enforce the necessary standards of quality and safety. For these reasons, it's argued, the industry must be kept under the microscope of government oversight.

Many of these same arguments used to be made about the importance of regulating the airline industry. What could be more basic than the need to ensure the safe travel of millions of passengers? How could private industry be trusted to provide that safety? But that argument failed the test of actual experience. After President Carter signed the Airline Deregulation Act some 40 years ago, the disruptive forces of the market went to work. Price competition came into play for the first time, and we saw start-ups such as Southwest and JetBlue gaining chunks of market share at the expense of higher-priced legacy airlines. Both route and schedule structures started to open up in response to consumer demand. And flying, which used to be primarily a means of transportation for the affluent, became a principal means of long-distance travel for just about everyone. And oh, by the way, the industry's safety record has improved enormously. The market, not the regulators, brought about these changes.

We're at that same juncture in the current state of health care. But in order to unleash the positive forces of the market, we need to systematically remove the regulatory and administrative barriers to change. We need to free up the economic human. Let it do the heavy lifting.

Here are the ESSENTIAL STEPS toward that end:

V-1 Get Rid of the Laws That Restrict Competition

Is competition a good thing? My own experience in working with health care providers throughout the country is that overall, they are a pretty competitive bunch. And they're competitive in the best sense. Physicians and other caregivers want the best clinical outcomes and patient satisfaction scores. Health care executives are obsessed with how they're trending on market share, because it's an objective measure of how consumers are responding to their programs and initiatives. Insurance executives have traditionally promoted products and product features in response to market needs and preferences.

As documented in Section I, however, there's been a progressive erosion of competition in health care over the years in both provider and insurance markets. This phenomenon has been largely due to payment and regulatory structures that have been ostensibly designed, in President Reagan's words, "to protect us from ourselves." These same structures have led to industry consolidation, less choice, and in some instances, cartel-like behavior.

Again, there seems to be the operative assumption on the part of legislators and regulators that the market is ignorant—that it doesn't have sufficient information to evaluate options and make prudent decisions. But as already discussed, this assumption is now null and void. With the unprecedented availability of Big Data and comparative analytics, the market now has access to the critical information—the market signals—that it needs in order to make rational purchase and consumption decisions. Going forward, we need to fully unleash this positive dynamic by revising or completely getting rid of the laws that artificially control the supply and pricing of health care. Specifically, we need to do the following:

1. *Repeal Certificate of Need laws*: As discussed in Chapter 7, Certificate of Need (CON) statutes are a legacy from a past era that has been perpetuated with the support of hospital associations and other trade groups who have the goal of keeping markets "organized". Which is to say that these vested interests have the unstated objective of curtailing competition. They restrict new entrants. And they can restrict the ability of existing providers to initiate new services that could be a source of competition to other established services in the market.

   The 35 states that have held on to these laws need to get rid of them. The right direction is captured by a fairly recent *Chicago Tribune* editorial regarding the ongoing mischief created by the Illinois Health Facilities and Services Review Board: "Trust the free markets. Bury the zombie board."[1] The same goes for all the remaining CON agencies. The sooner the better.

2. *Stop using COPA laws as shields against anti-trust*: Possibly nothing characterizes the schizophrenic nature of health policy more than the Certificate of Public Advantage (COPA) laws that still exist in a number of states. These laws, in effect, allow otherwise competing

health systems to enter into collaborative agreements to coordinate services for a defined population, usually Medicaid recipients. With COPA status, such systems can enter into business arrangements and share information that would normally be subject to Federal Trade Commission (FTC) enforcement action or private lawsuits. Although controversial from the beginning, especially in anti-trust enforcement circles, COPA provisions were given additional impetus by the Affordable Care Act and the emphasis on Accountable Care Organizations (ACOs) and other forms of collaboration.

The concurrent applications of FTC regulations, ACA provisions—and in many states, CON and COPA laws—blatantly underscore the inherent contradictions of health care policy. Service collaborations between disparate provider organizations either provide a sustainable advantage to the public, or not. If they do provide advantage, the organizations should be granted the latitude of legal merger. If they don't, they should be held to consistent, uniform anti-trust restrictions. The COPA laws are no more than a legal work-around to a mess that government has itself created. They need to be repealed.

3. *Ease the restrictions on retail clinics*: As discussed previously, the trend is for retail clinics, pharmacies, and supermarkets to bring basic medical services right to their customers. Although retail clinics are highly popular and have a proven safety track record, many states still have restrictions that block their implementation or severely restrict the scope of services that they can provide. This is despite the obvious accessibility and convenience advantages for customers, including rural areas that may lack other outpatient clinical resources. Not to mention cost. Walmart, for example, is now opening clinics in states where allowed, and is advertising a visit charge of $40—about one-half of the national average for a physician office visit.

The American Medical Association (AMA), to no one's surprise, has lobbied vigorously to keep these facilities out of the marketplace. The public needs to be better informed about this overall issue to get their legislators on board. We need to ease these restrictions and let the market decide how it wants to respond to this delivery alternative.

V-2 Remove Barriers to Market Pricing

It would seem to make intuitive sense that consumers should be able to access health care services on the basis of comparative cost. But in many instances there are restrictive barriers to doing just that. We need to remove these barriers through the following measures:

1. *Eliminate anti-steering provisions*: Health insurers often institute steering provisions designed to give enrollees incentives to use lower-cost health care providers. In many cases, however, health systems that have significant market share, and that consider themselves as *must-have* providers, insert anti-steering provisions in their contractual agreements with insurers. Anti-steering provisions effectively preclude insurers from steering enrollees to competing providers, even when such providers offer demonstrably superior value. These kinds of agreements ultimately lead to less market competition. Large health systems are given the advantage of greater volume/market share, and are somewhat insulated from price competition. In the end, consumers have fewer choices.

2. *Restrict the application of most-favored-nations clauses*: The most-favored-nations (MFN) clause is commonly used by large health plans to contractually preclude a provider system or network from offering the same or more favorable pricing to other insurance plans. Such stipulations

can set the stage for cartel-like behavior on the part of dominant health plans and provider systems. This can be harmful to competition in ways that effectively raise the cost of services for members of competing plans, with fewer options for narrow networks or tiered cost-sharing advantages.

Although MFN clauses are not, per se, illegal, they need to be scrutinized on a case-by-case basis and precluded by law when relevant provisions are inherently anti-competitive. The Department of Justice, as well as individual states, should continue to keep MFN provisions under the spotlight.

V-3 Eliminate Restrictions That Discourage Care Integration; Repeal the Stark Law

In 1989 Congress passed the Ethics in Patient Referrals Act, known today as the Stark law in recognition of the bill's sponsor, Congressman Pete Stark. In its original form, known as Stark I, the thrust of the statute was to ban physician self-referral of Medicare and other government payer patients for certain services—for example, lab, X-ray—when the physician has a financial arrangement involving those services. A Stark II revision expanded the statute in 1995, making the law extremely complex with a number of ambiguous exceptions. Any physician behavior that impinges on the boundaries of the law is a per se violation. Wrongful intent need not be proven, and whistleblowers have a significant financial incentive to alert officials under the False Claims Act.

There are three major problems with the Stark law. First, due to its sheer complexity and ambiguities, there are many unseen hazards for the otherwise scrupulous provider. Second, the very nature of the Act puts artificial restrictions on the integration and continuity of caregiver services. The Stark law perpetuates service fragmentation, and in this respect is antithetical to the principles of patient-centered car integration. Third, it's basically a holdover from the fee-for-service era, and effectively puts up a barrier to value-based reimbursement. It works against the concept of alternative pay-for-performance methodologies, including bundled payment models.

Regarding the matter of pay-for-performance, it should be noted that the Stark law not only discourages care coordination, but in many instances makes it virtually illegal. To draw a parallel, consider what the quality or cost of a consumer product—say, an automobile—might be like if the manufacturer of the basic body was not allowed to insource the engine, transmission, or other components. This is essentially what the Stark law prohibits health care providers from doing. Under ACA there's a provision for Stark waivers from fraud and abuse, but such waivers are limited, and in any case put providers in a gray area of uncertainty about what's legal and what's not.

Ideally, this law should be repealed. If we can't get rid of it, there should at least be a wholesale overhaul process that recognizes the need to support value-based payment methodologies.

As much or more than any other single piece of legislation, this law epitomizes the consequences of government's good intentions gone awry. It has all the ingredients: a seemingly virtuous rationale; a built-in distrust of the private sector of medicine; legislation that is labyrinthine in its complexity and application; a regulatory construct that actually works against the very goals of integrated medicine that the government is attempting to foster; and a guaranteed source of business and income for attorneys and many others in the MAC enterprise. In an interview with *The Wall Street Journal* reporters, Mr. Stark spoke for one constituency that is happy with the law: "I have every lawyer in town bowing gratitude to me for the work they got out of that law," he said.[2]

V-4 Change Laws to Make Drugs More Available, Less Expensive

Prescription drug costs are skyrocketing. For many they represent the single largest out-of-pocket health care cost. A large part of the reason for the high cost of drugs is because the pricing and availability of drugs have been adversely affected by outdated, dysfunctional regulations. We now need to realign policies and regulations in ways that make drugs more affordable, while providing manufacturers with the incentives that will support continued innovation. Specifically, we need to:

Remove the Artificial Protective Barriers to Market Competition

Since it takes an average of 10 years or so to bring a new drug to market, there's no argument that there should be certain protections from competing generic products for a reasonable period of time. But the already-lengthy periods of patent protections for approved drugs are easily (and frequently) extended by laws that prevent the FDA from approving a copy of an existing drug where there are actually no patents. Where patents do exist, drug companies can readily get extensions for extended testing to determine, for example, if the drug is suitable for children. Competing drugs can be, and often are, blocked by frivolous claims of patent infringement on the part of the originating company.

Another situation that doesn't get widespread publicity involves laws that prohibit the substitution of a prescribed drug or its generic equivalent from being dispensed, even in instances where the substitute drug is proven to be equally effective. This runs counter to any form of market logic, since the prescribing physician isn't affected by the higher cost of what he or she prescribes.

To make matters worse, Medicare is prohibited from directly negotiating drug prices. The pharmaceutical lobby has seen to that.

This is a complex topic, and the ultimate best-case solutions are beyond the scope of this book. But there are some fairly straightforward changes that could put prescription drugs into a more competitive market situation. One is to change the laws to (a) allow government programs (Medicare, Medicaid) to use clinical efficacy evaluations as a basis for directly negotiating prices with pharmaceutical companies; and (b) deploy reference pricing and restricted formularies to promote informed, disciplined market behavior.

Another measure would be to, in effect, give the public a return on its own investment. This is in reference to the fact that the pharmaceutical industry often relies on government-funded research as a basis for developing new drugs. The government needs to change its protocols for giving away the patents in such a way that the public, not just the drug companies, realize the benefits from these investments. This could be effective in the form of reduced drug pricing and/or shortened patent life.

Finally, we need to make information on the clinical efficacy and comparative effectiveness of prescription drugs more publicly available. Patients and their physicians should have the information to make the decisions on drugs that most meet their needs and where cost considerations are part of the equation. Patients should have the option of using health plan mail order options as an alternative to the often higher-priced retail pharmacies. State laws that pose restrictions on mail order for the benefit of local retailers should be repealed.

Streamline the Approval Processes for Generic Drugs

Generic drugs are cheaper. They are affordable to any number of people who would otherwise not have access to treatments that could be highly beneficial. And they provide the discipline of market competition that can have a salutatory effect on the pricing of their original equivalents as well as other look-alikes that come along. The approval of generic drugs should not be an extended process. They're not experimental. The only concern from a testing standpoint is whether or not they're equivalent to their brand name equivalents in terms of quality purity, and effectiveness.

Why then, does the FDA continue to have an enormous backlog of generic drugs awaiting approval? Why does it often take four years or more? Government officials point to the need for additional funding and staff resources. And to be fair, the FDA more recently has been making some strides in reducing the backlog for so-called Abbreviated New Drug Application (ANDA) drugs. But we have a long way to go. The expanded availability of generic drugs is a logical and attainable solution to at least mitigating the escalating cost of drugs in the U.S.

Enact "Right-to-Try" Legislation for Terminally Ill Patients

Over a million people in the U.S. die from a terminal illness each year. Many are logical candidates to participate in clinical trials and potentially benefit from experimental drugs. As it now stands, terminally ill patients can petition the FDA for permission to use experimental drugs that have passed the Phase I level of clinical trials. But FDA rules restrict and delay access to innovative and promising new treatments. For many who finally do gain access, it's often so delayed that it winds up being too late.

As this is written there are two right-to-try bills pending in Congress that could pave the way for many terminally ill patients to gain access to experimental drugs as a last resort. We need to pass this legislation.

V-5 Modify Rules in Order to Ease the Administrative Burden on Physicians

The burdens of complying with Centers for Medicare and Medicaid Services (CMS) reporting requirements for such programs as the Physician Quality Reporting System (PQRS) and value-based modifier (VBM) requirements are consuming ever-increasing amounts of the average physician's time and energy, and are diverting attention away from the focus on patient care. How much time? A recent study by the Dartmouth–Hitchcock health system shows that a representative cross-section of physicians spend nearly one-half of their time on EHR data entry and other administrative duties, and only a little over a quarter of their time on direct patient care.[3] Other recent studies have found similar patterns.

All of this not only detracts from patient care, but in some cases leads to physician burnout. Studies conducted by Mayo Clinic and others point to increasing levels of dissatisfaction linked to administrative burdens and frustrations with technology.[4] Timewise, the upswing in professional dissatisfaction has coincided with much of the implementation of electronic health records and related administrative complexities posed by MACRA (Medicare Access and CHIP Reauthorization Act) and other government-imposed requirements. There's already evidence that these frustrations are leading some doctors to reduce the time they are spending on clinical work, or in some instances retire early or leave the profession to do other work. Surprising to some, the studies on physician dissatisfaction report that it's actually higher in large practices and in practices owned by health systems. This may seem counterintuitive, since physicians in larger practice settings typically have access to more administrative support. Based on my own conversations with doctors in these settings, I believe that much of this dissatisfaction has to do with the feelings of loss of control and professional autonomy.

What can be done to improve this situation? On the good news front, CMS has punted on the implementation of the Stage 3 Meaningful Use requirements, which should give clinicians at least some temporary relief from administrative overload. Here are some additional changes that should be made:

1. *Simplify rules and reporting requirements*: Given the timing overlay of all the requirements being imposed (e.g., APMs, merit-based incentive payment systems), reporting systems need to be designed so that data inputs for one report are automatically entered for other reporting purposes. At the same time, there is a need to develop consistent technical requirements for EHR certification.
2. *Eliminate the interface walls between EHR systems*: Vendors have purposely built in barriers to interoperability between the various EHR systems. We need to ramp up oversight and put in the sanctions as necessary to get rid of vendor-designed roadblocks.
3. *Reduce structured requirements to make data entry more efficient and relevant*: For EHR entries beyond the structured data that are strictly required by CMS, we need to allow for more efficient forms of input (e.g., dictation, free-text entry). There also needs to be a simplification and streamlining of protocols in ways that medical assistants and other non-physician staff can take on more of the administrative responsibilities.

V-6 Reform Medical Malpractice Laws

As cited previously, the cost of defensive medicine has been estimated to account for about one out of every four dollars spent. The cost of medical practice liability coverage has reached a point where many physicians have restricted the scope of their practices, and a number have left medicine altogether.

Numerous national malpractice reform measures have been proposed over the years at both federal and state levels. Going forward we need to tackle at the very least the following basic remedies:

1. *Cap non-economic damages*: As it stands now, there's no federal limitation on awards for non-economic damages, which include pain and suffering. We need to cap non-economic damages at a reasonable level. As of this writing, there's a proposal pending in the U.S. Congress (the Protecting Access to Care Act) to put this cap in place at $250,000. We need to move forward with this or similar legislation. At the same time we need to bar plaintiffs from including providers in product liability suits involving drugs and medical devices.

2. *Establish uniform statutes of limitations*: Many states have very loose statute of limitations requirements on the window of time in which a claimant can bring suit after an injury or the discovery of an injury. As part of any overhaul provisions, we need to put in place a reasonable statute of limitations at the national level. The aforementioned federal legislation would put a three-year limitation on any action after the injury has been incurred, or one-year after its discovery.

3. *Put limits on attorney contingency fees*: One of the problems with medical malpractice claims is that it's often the plaintiff's attorney that winds up with the lion's share of any settlement. We need to put reasonable limitations on contingency fees that are paid to the lawyers. California has a statute in place that could serve as a national template. In that state, the attorney's contingency fee is limited to 40% of the first $50,000 recovered, 33% of the next $50,000, and 15% of any settlement amount that exceeds $600,000.

   Needless to say, these types of reforms are not easy to pass. But they are an important piece of the overall transformation process in the Next Curve. This issue needs to be given more visibility and debate in the public forum.

References

1. Editorial Board, Trust the free markets. Bury the zombie board, *Chicago Tribune*, May 6, 2016. http://www.chicagotribune.com/news/opinion/editorials/ct-illinois-health-board-schmidt-rauner-corruption-edit-0509-jm-20160506-story.html.
2. J. Carreyou, J. Adamy, How Medicare Self-Referral Thrives on Loophole, *The Wall Street Journal*, October 22, 2014. https://www.wsj.com/articles/how-medicare-self-referral-thrives-on-loophole-1414031401.
3. C. Sinsky, L. Colligan et al., Allocation of physician time in ambulatory practice: A time and motion study in 4 specialties, *Annals of Internal Medicine*, December 6, 2016. http://annals.org/aim/article-abstract/2546704/allocation-physician-time-ambulatory-practice-time-motion-study-4-specialties.
4. T. Shanafelt et al., Changes in burnout and satisfaction with work-life balance in physicians and the general US working population between 2011 and 2014, *Mayo Clinic Proceedings*, 90(12), 1600–1613, December 2015.

Chapter 16

Positioning Strategies for the New Future

"I must be willing to give up what I am in order to become what I will be."

—Albert Einstein, 1879–1955

CHAPTER OVERVIEW

- A new market ecosystem is restructuring the health care product, price, and delivery landscape.
- Consumers, not providers, will be defining value in the Next Curve.
- Health care leaders need to set forth a functional blueprint for the new future that starts with the customer and is based on true value differentiators.
- Finally, we need to unleash the economic human— the spirit of health care.

A New Market Ecosystem

What is health care? Think of it as a product. Simply stated, it's *health*: the prevention of disease and the health status improvement of individuals and communities. And it's *care*: the diagnosis, treatment, and restoration of people with disease- and injury-related conditions.

These definitions seem basic. But if you look at the existing industry structure, it would be understandable if you think of health care as a delivery system, an insurance company, or, for that matter, a government agency. These organizations are no longer just about the support of the primary mission of health and care. They have evolved to the point where *infrastructure* has become an end unto itself. It now defines the industry.

This brings to mind the history of certain other business models. Take Kodak, for example. There are few corporate blunders as mind-boggling as Kodak's failure to embrace digital imaging, a technology it invented. The company's leaders had two basic blind spots. First, they didn't seem to comprehend that they were in the *image* business, not the film manufacturing business. Second, they were unable to see digital photography for the disruptive technology that it was. Even as late as 2007, the company launched a marketing campaign touting film products and dismissing digital technology as a "passing fad". Other companies, as well as entire industries, have fallen into the same trap of not understanding just what their business really is. Blockbuster is an historic example. Now any number of news media, bookstores, and retail chains are facing a questionable future for the same reason.

Health care is in a similar situation today. While the traditional players are focused on making incremental changes to the existing industry model, disruptive forces are at work making some of the most basic structural features of this model totally obsolete. As we've explored, Big Data and all of its downstream analytics are radically transforming the manner in which disease is identified, diagnosed, and treated. With the increasing availability and transparency of cost and outcomes data, value is becoming more tangible and quantifiable. Going back to the basic principles of the Next Curve, we're entering a new era where value is defined, measured, compared, and rewarded by the market, based on available options and pricing signals. An informed, rational market—the economic human—is the agent of change in this new future.

What we're seeing is a new market ecosystem. The recent announcement by Amazon, Berkshire Hathaway, and JPMorgan Chase that they are getting into the health care business is a major sign of how the industry is changing. For health industry players who are stuck in the First and Second Curves, this development may signal the demise of the proverbial canary in the mine. While the full dimensions of this and similar industry disruptions can't be precisely foretold at this time, we do know that this fusion of dollars, expertise, and technology—combined with the commitment to improve the health of a million-plus individuals—will be an industry-changing phenomenon.

In any case, the manner in which services will be structured and delivered in the Next Curve will pose a major challenge for the typical hospital or health system. Medicine will be transitioning away from the traditional institutional setting. Consumers will be demanding ease of access and patient-friendly service platforms. Services will increasingly be delivered in high-tech outpatient centers, mini-hospitals, and retail centers, as well as the home setting. There will be a continued blurring of the lines of distinction between insurers, providers, and employers.

How services are priced will be another major disruption. With rising co-pays and deductibles, the market will become increasingly sensitive to pricing and price variations. The current pricing model, with its overlay of artificial constructs that include shadow pricing, formula-driven cost accounting, and largely invisible forms of cross-subsidization, will become increasingly irrelevant. The newer entrants into the health care market—the disruptors—won't be locked into these arcane pricing methodologies. They'll be looking at actual *process costing*. The disruptors can easily undercut the price points of the traditional provider market. This will force everyone to go back and analyze the true costs of production, and start to take their pricing cues from the market.

The implications of this new market ecosystem are staggering. Health care institutions are a high-fixed cost business. Think of their economic balance as a teeter-totter with fixed costs as the fulcrum. Any change in marginal costs or marginal revenues will significantly tip the balance one way or another. For a hospital, a seemingly small shift in market share, occupancy rates, or pricing methodology can dramatically affect the institution's economics. Further, the traditional health institution is highly dependent on patient channels that involve the vertical referral chain of primary care services and outpatient services.

Together, these factors make the health system highly vulnerable to any form of disruption. Walmart medical revenues in a given local market may be objectively small in comparison to those of established health systems. But any loss of market share on the part of a large, campus-based system can have a significant impact on that organization's operating performance. The traditional health care organization—particularly the large, campus-based health provider system—will need to either significantly transform its business model or face the prospect of declining utilization and deteriorating financial position. Much like the general department store in today's market.

Consumers Will Define Value

Consumers will be defining value in the Next Curve. They will continue to seek the best possible clinical care and outcomes, but at the same time will be looking for value in the form of cost, convenience, and provider connectivity and engagement.

As the leaders of today's health care institutions consider what it will take for their organizations to be successful in this evolving market, they should consider three basic questions:

1. How will your *customers* define value?
2. In what ways will your competition—particularly the market disruptors—exploit this concept of value?
3. What specific strategies and business models will position your organization not just as a responder, but as a *leader and disruptor* in this evolving, consumer-driven market?

In addressing these questions, it's important to consider that the consumer's perception of value, as well as his or her value-seeking behavior, will vary depending on the types of services being sought. In the new future of the Next Curve, there will be less and less *global loyalty* to a given provider system for any and all services.

In order to understand this changing market dynamic, it's instructive to look at health care services by grouping them into three broad categories:

Category 1: The Routine Stuff

This category includes the bumps, bruises, sore throats, and other hazards of everyday life. It also includes basic diagnostic and treatment services, such as a routine laboratory test or mammography, or a simple outpatient surgical procedure. It's a significant part of total health care expenses and is the type of provider encounter that the majority of people experience in any given year. Because of the volume potential and relative lack of complexity, this is the category of services that the disruptors are targeting.

Category 1 services are the closest things to commodities that we have in health care. And much like other commodity-type services, consumers put a value premium on two factors: convenience and price. The non-traditional players in this market—whether it's Walmart, CVS, a tele-health company, or other retail providers—will make certain that the market knows what their service features and prices are. Can health systems or private physician offices ignore this pitch? Absolutely not. Traditional providers will have to be transparent about their service responsiveness and prices. And their prices will have to be market-competitive, and not determined by administered formulas.

Category 2: Disease- and Condition-Related Care

This category consists of injury- or disease-specific treatment at various levels and stages of care. It includes specialty and sub-specialty physician care, inpatient hospitalization, and ongoing rehabilitation and treatment. This is the category of care that we would not usually consider to be particularly price-sensitive, or where patients are likely to be doing much window shopping. When it comes to this category of care, patients have traditionally deferred to the judgment of their referring doctors.

But this consumer orientation breaks down in the new future of the Next Curve. In much the same way as the routine care in Category 1, the services in this category—especially procedure-specific outpatient services—are becoming increasingly sensitive to factors related to price, location, and overall convenience. This is particularly true for the many patients who are digging more deeply into their pockets due to rising deductible levels. People are looking at options. They are comparing prices. We can expect to see the continued growth on the part of free-standing facilities and various new entrants in this segment. Here again, the traditional health provider system can't ignore the potential impact of the disruptors in this market segment.

Category 3: Health and Wellness—Engaged Partnership

This is the panoply of personalized services and technologies that link health and wellness. Increasingly, consumers want their health providers to understand and connect their health status—the quantified self—with digital health and overall prevention and wellness coordination. With the evolution of wearable technology and availability of real-time information, this digital body narrative can alert both consumer and caregivers to potential health issues, which, in turn, can trigger preventive measures. This information can also be of major value in developing treatment and recovery protocols.

This category of care is the real game-changer. Clearly, it's a segment that's being targeted by various technology firms (e.g., FitBit, Apple). It's also a wide-open opportunity for other evolving disruptors, such as the fusion models that are linking together retail medicine, pharmaceuticals, and insurance.

Figure 16.1 highlights the key value differentiators by category of care.

These differentiators put the large, capital-based health care system in a vulnerable position, since these organizations are locked into rigid infrastructures and a high overhead cost structure. From a mission standpoint, most not-for-profit institutions have an ongoing commitment to provide certain services that don't contribute to operating margin. At the same time, they are highly vulnerable to new entrants and single-play providers that can undercut their pricing for more profitable services.

For the Category 1 *routine stuff* services, the large health system will need to be fully responsive to consumer demands for convenience and market-competitive pricing. Consumers will be increasingly aware of the other options that are

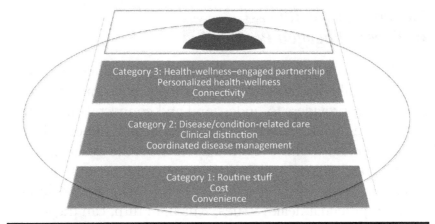

Category 3: Health-wellness–engaged partnership
Personalized health-wellness
Connectivity

Category 2: Disease/condition-related care
Clinical distinction
Coordinated disease management

Category 1: Routine stuff
Cost
Convenience

Figure 16.1   Value differentiation in the Next Curve.

available to them. In particular, the growing share of the market with high-deductible insurance plans will be looking for low-cost alternatives for this level of care.

For Category 2 services, consumers will continue to orient to traditional campus-based hospital settings for complex surgeries and other high-end specialty and subspecialty services. But much of what falls in the Category 2 segment consists of services that can readily be provided in lower-cost, user-friendly physicians' offices, medical malls, and mini-hospitals. Health systems that haven't done so already will need to challenge their existing delivery infrastructure and transition to a more distributed, accessible and patient-friendly delivery platform.

The Category 3 services pose both a big threat but also a major opportunity for the established health system. To the extent that large health systems can effectively link health care and wellness in a personalized way, this engaged partnership can be that "magic glue" that binds their customer base to them. It can effectively raise the switching costs for the patient. This is a critical positioning strategy. Given their overall cost structure, large health provider systems will never be able to match the price points of single-stage providers for certain services. But if they can nurture the patient relationship in an engaged partnership manner, they can effectively raise the switching costs for the patient to a point where the patient is more likely to remain loyal to the system.

This patient/customer partnership has to be real. It not only must give the consumer tangible value, but this value must be of such a nature that it puts up entry barriers to competitors. Failure to do this is a recipe for failure. I'm reminded of an earlier era where a major airline, United Airlines, attempted to vertically integrate the travel business with a host of air routes, hotels, car rental agencies, and so on, under a new corporate label, Allegis. As the name implied, the strategy was to lock in the *allegiance* of the customer base. But the strategy failed. Customers could find no tangible value in the connections, and they became annoyed at the idea of being *steered* to services and brands that they didn't really want. Health care organizations need to avoid making this same mistake.

Positioning for the Next Curve

The leaders of today's health care institutions must have a clearly defined vision and direction for how they need to position their organization as we head into the Next Curve. As highlighted in Figure 16.2, the strategic thrust of the health care system will need to make the shift from what has essentially been a *compliance focus* in the Second Curve, to what now needs to be a concentrated *market focus*.

As part of this market focus, repositioning strategies need to take into full account the shift from disease-specific, episodic care to whole-person care and condition-related care coordination across the span of treatment, recovery, and lifestyle enhancement. At the same time, there needs to be a full recognition that the movement toward *value* in the Second Curve has been driven by

Figure 16.2   Strategic focus in the Next Curve.

administered pricing and standardized value measures. In the Next Curve, value will increasingly be determined by actual costs, market-driven pricing, and consumer preferences.

So how should today's health care leaders begin positioning their organizations for the Next Curve? Here's a five-step trans-formational change agenda that I have shared with my clients, and that I believe is a relevant roadmap to the new future for almost any health care institution:

1. *Make the customer the primary focus*: Strategic plan-ning in health care has often been centered on pro-vider interests. This orientation needs to be turned around, with the consumer now as the central focus. This will require a research-based understanding of consumer needs and service-seeking behavior as it relates to such factors as access, quality, user-friendliness, and cost.

2. *Find the true value differentiators*: Health care decision-makers can safely assume that most of their competition will be making more or less the same selling points. So what's needed is to identify and develop those dif-ferentiators that are truly unique and sustainable—to

find that secret sauce. Those differentiators should be "sticky", which is to say that they should have the effect of locking in customer loyalty such that there are both tangible and emotional costs to switching to another provider.

3. *Avoid the "curve trap"; be your own disruptor*: As we proceed headlong into the new and dynamic future, it will be incumbent on health leaders to have in place a very defined blueprint—a functional vision—that not only defines the future state destination, but lays out the very specific structures that will need to be in place in order to actualize this blueprint. In so doing, there needs to be a conscious intellectual separation of *what is* from *what needs to be*. This is another way of saying that organizational leaders need to avoid the *curve trap* of trying to protect current strategies or infrastructure, when the market may be moving in an altogether different direction.

4. *Erase the traditional segment boundaries*: As health leaders think about positioning in the new future, they shouldn't be bound by traditional industry definitions of relevant service segments and business models. They need to understand what the relevant *product* is. This understanding can open the door to creative and mutually beneficial partnerships with organizations in vertically related parts of the value chain. In some cases, it may involve a fusion of functions and institutions that profoundly change the structure and direction of existing organizational models.

5. *Make value transparent*: Clinical outcome, pricing, and patient satisfaction metrics should be objectively quantified and freely shared with consumer and purchaser markets. Cost and pricing determinations should be objectively based on the actual costs of production, not on administratively determined formulas.

Unleashing the Spirit of Health Care

In the course of my work spanning several decades I have had the opportunity to meet and work with literally thousands of health care professionals representing a diverse body of health care institutions throughout the country. It's been a privilege to get to know these individuals and the organizations they represent. And to learn from them.

Among other things, I have been impressed with what I call the *spirit of health care.* This isn't a tangible thing, and in many ways it's hard to describe. But what I have observed in the many caregivers and organizations that I have come to know is a near-universal dedication to mission and to doing the *just right* things for patients and communities served. In this regard, there's a genuine alignment of values that make health care a somewhat unique sector in our society.

Another aspect of the health care industry culture that has impressed me is the ability and willingness of caregivers and those in leadership positions to make logic-based decisions that are ultimately in the best interests of the constituencies they serve. Health care organizations are a microcosm of society. They include people with widely varying points of view on almost any topic. And there are the politics of vested interests that come with every department and clinical discipline. But what I have found is that if there's an alignment of values and objectives, and if people are presented with fact-based analyses and the comparative outcomes of meaningful options, they will more often than not unify around a sound course of direction. The spirit of health care is embedded in this culture.

On a broader societal scale, we need to invoke this spirit in the Next Curve. The core theme of this book has followed two fundamental precepts: First, that as a society, our values as they relate to health care are more aligned than is generally recognized. And second, that the informed market and the economic human needs to be the driving force of change. Not the politicians. And not our old pal, MAC. Let's send him off to a not-so-early retirement.

Unleash the spirit of health care. *Homo economicus.*

Appendix: How We Got Here—A Brief History of Health Care in the U.S.

So how did we get to the current state of health care in the U.S.? In this appendix we'll do some time travel back through a history of health policy extending over the past 100+ years.

1910: Taft, the American Medical Association, and Putting Limits on Physician Supply

Among developed countries, the U.S. currently has one of the lowest physician-to-population ratios (2.5 per 1,000 population, compared to the average of 3.0 for OECD countries), and one of the lowest annual physician consultations per capita (3.9 per 1,000, compared to the 6.3 average for OECD).[1] What most people don't realize is that physician supply in the U.S. has been tightly controlled through a partnership of government and medical lobby interests that dates back to 1910. (Yes, MAC [medical-administrative complex] was alive and well over a century ago.) At that time there was a move by the Taft administration, with the advocacy of the American Medical

Association (AMA), to shut down a number of medical schools and reduce class sizes.

The AMA subsequently lobbied the states to aggressively regulate medical licensure and influence state subsidies for medical education. Based on this command and control model, the Graduate Medical Education National Advisory Committee (GMENAC) was chartered in 1976 by the Secretary, Department of Health, Education and Welfare (now the Department of Health and Human Services [DHHS]) to determine future physician needs by specialty, based on population and geography. Although GMENAC was an ad hoc effort and subsequently decommissioned in 1980, its recommendations have been widely used as a reference for funding education even to this day. The result has been a consistently restrictive approach that has limited physician supply, creating an imbalance between supply and demand in many geographic locales.

Given current physician demographics and the aging of the U.S. population as a whole (and associated increases in physician demand), we face a significant shortfall of physicians going forward. According to the latest projections from the American Association of Medical Colleges, the U.S. will have a shortfall of somewhere between 41,000 and 105,000 physicians by 2030.[2]

1929: Blue Cross Blue Shield Comes to Life

Although not a legislative initiative, the founding of Blue Cross Blue Shield was a seminal event in our health care history. Initiated as a non-profit prepaid plan by Baylor University in Dallas, the introduction of the plan was created as a non-profit alternative to commercial insurance plans for teachers. The concept of prepaid, non-profit health care coverage was widely embraced by a receptive public, particularly as gaps in health coverage grew due to the effect of the Great Depression.

The importance of Blue Cross Blue Shield in our cultural mind-set toward health care coverage can't be overstated. It was the precursor to the rapid expansion of employer-based insurance. It contributed to the evolving concept that health care should be made available to anyone who needs it.

1935: The Social Security Act and a Stepping Stone toward Medicare

Medical benefits were not included in the Social Security Act signed by President Roosevelt in 1935. But the seeds were planted. There was, in fact, a great deal of discussion at the time about amending the bill to include a national health benefit. This idea was later picked up by President Truman, who made attempts to include medical care for the aged in his Fair Deal Program.

All of this provided the impetus and foundation for the Social Security Act of 1965 establishing Medicare and Medicaid programs. The Social Security Act played a major role in setting the stage for a greatly expanded government role in our lives. It led to the whole idea of using payroll withholding to pay for employee benefits.

World War II and Employer-Based Health Insurance

Prior to World War II people either had their own health insurance or, in many instances, paid out-of-pocket directly to providers. Back then, insurance was truly insurance, which is to say that it provided coverage for just the major events, with individuals paying for all other care. During the war the government was highly concerned about inflation and instituted wage and price controls to avoid a scenario of hyperinflation. As a concession to labor groups, the War Labor Board took the step of exempting employer-based health benefits from wage controls and income tax. This historical circumstance laid the foundation for the employer-based health insurance model that prevails to this day, with both employers and employees receiving full tax deduction for health plan costs.

1945: The McCarran-Ferguson Act and the Legalization of the Insurance Monopoly

President Roosevelt took the step of exempting health insurance companies from most federal regulations, including antitrust laws. This step also gave the states carte blanche latitude to set standards for coverage and effectively limit health plans to in-state coverage only.

The effect of this Act was to impose state-mandated coverage requirements that could raise the cost of premiums enormously, and at the same time prevent residents of one state from shopping around for plans in other states where products have less onerous coverage requirements and are more price competitive. Some states like New York, for example, have guaranteed-issue and community-rating provisions that keep younger, healthy people out of the market. It's not currently possible for out-of-state plans to offer competing products to these individuals.

1946: The Hill–Burton Act, Reduced Competition, and Full Barrels of Park

The Hospital Survey and Construction Act, otherwise known as Hill–Burton, was passed to help fund the construction of hospitals using grants and guaranteed loans. Needless to say, it was highly supported by the states and construction trades. The target was to achieve 4.5 beds per 1,000 population, which at that time was deemed "adequate" to take care of the hospitalization needs of a given locale.

Hill–Burton fueled a huge amount of construction until its demise in the 1990s. Some of this construction was objectively needed, but much was not. States were required to have plans to demonstrate need. But hospitals and construction trades found it easy to game the rules to meet the states' statutory requirements. Anti-trust restrictions did not apply to hospitals built or expanded under this program. Construction costs and cost-inflation in the hospital segment became rampant.

This program had the effect of radically changing the health care infrastructure in the U.S. Some areas were overbuilt with hospital beds right from the start. Subsequent changes in health technology and the shift from inpatient care to outpatient services have since resulted in over-bedded situations in many communities. Whereas the target was 4.5 beds per 1,000 population when the law was passed, many markets can now accommodate demand with less than 2.5 beds per 1,000 people. An empty bed—and there are many of those throughout the country—has a standing cost that is roughly two-thirds that of an occupied bed. We are still living with the long-term effects of this legislation.

1954: Tax-Free Employee Health Benefits

In 1954 the federal government codified into law the provision that employers could provide health insurance benefits to workers tax-free. This made permanent an earlier, World War II ruling that made such benefits non-taxable. Other than the later passage of Medicare-Medicaid, there is probably no other single measure that has done more to shape the direction of U.S. health care than this ruling. For employees who receive it, the pre-tax benefit amounts to a very substantial discount from what people who don't have it must pay for health insurance.

1960: Kerr-Mills and the Road to Medicare and Medicaid

The Kerr-Mills Act extended health care benefits to the medically indigent, including people aged 65 and over, as well as to other uninsured or under-insured individuals. Based on a matching formula at the state level, Kerr-Mills would later become one of the structural building blocks of the Medicaid program. Because it was embedded in the public assistance program structure, it was widely regarded as a welfare program and had the stigma of public assistance. But it served the important purpose of laying some of the groundwork for the passage of Medicare and Medicaid in 1965.

1965: Medicare, Medicaid, and a New Era of Health Care

The nationalization of health care was formalized with the passage of the Social Security Amendment of 1965, which provided health insurance for the elderly and the poor. Funded by the federal government and by payroll taxes, Medicare provides health coverage to individuals aged 65 and over for hospitalizations, physician services, and drug costs. Medicaid, funded at both state and federal levels, provides health coverage to certain low-income individuals.

Together, Medicare and Medicaid have radically transformed the health industry landscape, not to mention the federal budget. However well intended, these programs have been and continue to be an ever-expanding sponge for federal dollars and sadly, are a fertile ground for waste and for fraud committed by physicians, hospitals, and patients. Collectively, Medicare and Medicaid together now account for 25% of our federal tax dollars.

1971: The Perloff Report and Seeds of the Future

Few individuals today are aware of or will recall the Perloff Report. Otherwise known as Ameriplan, this was a proposal set forth by think tanks, working in conjunction with the American Hospital Association, to fundamentally restructure our health care delivery system. The actual report has been lost in the dust bins of history, but the overall recommendations of this initiative provided much of the intellectual DNA for the later evolution of health care provider systems. The Perloff Report called for a total restructuring of our health care delivery system into geographic districts, with integrated health care corporations responsible for providing care to defined populations. The seeds were planted for the later formation of integrated health delivery systems and, under Obamacare, the development of Accountable Care Organizations.

1974: Certificate of Need and a History of Malfeasance and Corruption

This legislation, known as the National Health Planning and Resources Development Act, was passed during the Nixon administration. It was a belated recognition that the Hill–Burton Act and other measures, intended to encourage the construction of health facilities, had resulted in overbuilding, duplications, and excessive hospital costs in many parts of the country.

The intent of the legislation was to coordinate health planning processes at federal, state, and local levels to determine health resource needs. This was done through so-called Certificate of Need (CON) processes, whereby health institutions were required to submit proposed bed additions or other capital projects for review if they exceeded a certain dollar threshold. States were mandated to implement their own CON processes, consistent with federal requirements.

The CON processes failed to meet their objectives. Even worse, powerful interests in many states manipulated the system to protect hospital turf and bed franchises. Health systems with legitimate needs for project approvals were often denied based on artificial or politicized criteria.

The federal government repealed the CON mandate in 1986, and some states immediately discontinued their programs. But as of now, some 35 states still have some form of CON legislation. This status quo is supported by powerful health industry interests who continue to use it as a regulatory barrier to competition and innovation.

1974: Employment Retirement Income Security Act and the Expanding Role of Federal Government

Most people associate the Employment Retirement Income Security Act (ERISA) with pension benefits. But it has had a major impact on health care through provisions that pre-empt or override state health laws as they pertain to employer health plans. Employers who purchase coverage from insurance companies are regulated directly at the federal level and indirectly at the state level. Self-insured plans are regulated strictly at the federal level. In any case, ERISA has put the federal government in a powerful role as it relates to policies and regulations for such plans.

1983: The Prospective Payment System Lays the Groundwork for Value-Based Reimbursement

By the late 1970s there was a growing realization that health care costs were headed off the tracks. Hill–Burton had led to a huge expansion of hospital capacities in the U.S. The growth of employer-based plans and Medicare and Medicaid had resulted in unprecedented levels of demand for both inpatient and outpatient services. There was little incentive for health providers *not* to build new hospitals or expansions, since reimbursement from Medicare and other payers was based on a *cost-plus* methodology. By the same token, there was no incentive to monitor utilization or the effective use of health resources. A dollar spent by a provider was a dollar-plus reimbursed.

The Social Security Amendments of 1983 started the ball rolling in a different direction. With this legislation, the Prospective Payment System (PPS) was introduced, whereby the method of Medicare payment for a specific service was based on a classification scheme of diagnosis-related groups (DRGs). With this new scheme, payment was no longer based, for example, on the number of days of inpatient stay, but instead was calculated through an average of costs reflecting a broader universe of hospitals treating patients with the same illness. This put in place the current model, whereby Medicare pays a set price for the collective services provided; for example, in an inpatient hospital stay, regardless of actual resources consumed. The amount to be reimbursed is determined and set by Centers for Medicare and Medicaid Services (CMS) prospectively. This change laid the groundwork for the various value-based payment methodologies that are evolving today.

1989: The Medicare Catastrophic Coverage Act and Lessons Unlearned

The Medicare Catastrophic Coverage Act capped the annual out-of-pocket costs of co-payments for hospitalization, and paid for limited prescription drug coverage. The problem is that it was "help" that was literally inflicted on recipients. A premium expansion that was calculated using a sliding scale based on income, so that the more affluent seniors—many of whom already had separate catastrophic coverage—were asked to pick up the lion's share of the tab. The people who didn't need the coverage wound up floating the subsidy boat for others.

This situation came to a head in 1989 when the Democratic Chairman of the Ways and Means Committee, Dan Rostenkowski, was mobbed by senior citizens in his own Chicago voting district who blocked his car and forced him to flee on foot. Most of the provisions of the law were repealed soon thereafter. For those paying attention, this debacle could have provided valuable insights into how some members of the public would react to Hillarycare, and later, the Affordable Care Act.

1993: Stark and Anti-Kickback Restrictions

The so-called Stark law, introduced as Stark I in the 1990 legislation and subsequently revised as Stark II in the 1993 act, was designed to prevent the conflict of interests that physicians may have in referring patients to entities (e.g., laboratories, therapy centers) in which they have financial interests. While intended to prevent self-dealing and artificially high costs, the applicable laws have become very complex and difficult for physicians to understand without extensive training. In many cases, they have actually discouraged doctors from giving discounts to poorer, self-pay patients.

The impacts of the Stark laws have become especially relevant in the context of the current trend toward bundled care pricing and value-based payment models. By putting restrictions on the ability of caregivers to refer patients to certain providers, limitations have been put on their ability to make judgments and come to the best clinical decisions regarding the use of other physician and technological resources. It's one of the reasons for the fragmented delivery model that exists today.

1993: Hillarycare and the Limitations of Academically Engineered Policy

Immediately after his inauguration, President Clinton appointed his wife, Hillary Clinton, as chair of a President's Task Force on National Health Reform. Although the resulting plan went down in defeat, it planted many of the seeds for the later passage of Obamacare. It was also a prognosticator of some of the polarization of public sentiment about Obamacare.

Officially known as the Health Security Act, the key feature of the proposed plan was universal health coverage. The plan would have given insurance companies control over health care providers, with doctors working in group practices that would be set up as health maintenance organizations. The Act would have required that everyone be enrolled in qualified health plans to be offered by all businesses with more than 5,000 employees or by regional health alliances to be set up by each state. These alliances would purchase insurance coverage for individuals and would set fee rates for providers. Subsidies would then be provided for those who could not afford coverage. The plan also would have set up a national health board to oversee the quality of health care services provided.

Many people had basic problems with the core feature of Hillarycare. This was the provision that insurance companies would in effect run the show, and could dictate to both consumers and providers the types and levels of services that could be provided. Other people, including many Democrats, were unhappy with the proposal because it didn't go so far as to incorporate a single payer proposal.

The Hillarycare proposal, although very different from Obamacare in many respects, was a prelude to the shortcomings of the Affordable Care Act in one very important respect. It was the product of academic engineering, closed-door sessions, and a lack of input from people who lived in the real world of health care. Hillarycare did not get the political traction it needed, and wound up dead on arrival.

2010: The Affordable Care Act and an Unaffordable New Direction

The Patient Protection and Affordable Care Act, usually referred to as either the Affordable Care Act or Obamacare, has in many respects been the biggest change to U.S. health care since the passage of Medicare and Medicaid. With most provisions still in effect as of this writing, the ACA was intended to expand health plan coverage to the uninsured and reduce health care costs. This has been done through the introduction of insurance mandates, subsidies, and exchanges. The law, in effect, has required health plans to accept all applicants, cover a specified range of conditions, and be priced at the same rates regardless of any pre-existing conditions. The ACA has stipulated that young adults under the age of 26 be covered as part of their family plan.

Obamacare has failed to meet its goals primarily because the insurance products are out of sync with what people want or are willing to pay for. It has boxed insurers into providing very expensive policies with more coverage than many individuals need, want, or can afford. Despite the mandates, many individuals, particularly younger people, aren't buying the product. The penalties for not getting coverage are relatively low compared with the high premiums and the unlikely probability of getting sick.

To make matters worse, people have had the option of signing up *after* they became ill and need financial assistance. The plans can't exclude people with pre-existing conditions. All of this has had the combined effect of reducing the total premium dollars while skewing the risk pool toward a less healthy population. It is an insurance model that has defied the laws of actuarial physics.

That is not to say that Obamacare does not have some good features. The stipulation that health plans cannot exclude individuals on the basis of pre-existing conditions has put the spotlight on a long-standing problem. And there has been, at long last, recognition of the need for more proactive population health initiatives, which remains a promising (but mostly unfulfilled) objective to this day.

2011: Bundled Payment and Another Step toward Value

Designed by CMS as a modification to the Prospective Payment System, the bundled payment methodology provides a lump-sum payment for services provided by the hospital, hospital physicians, and aftercare providers for a period of up to 90 days after the patient has left the hospital. The intent is to provide a financial incentive for all caregivers to work closely together to coordinate care. Although it didn't get a lot of public press coverage at the time, this provision has had a major (and positive) impact on the delivery and economics of health care services.

2018 and Forward: Lessons Learned?

You may be asking, "What's the relevance of legislation going back some 100+ years? What does that have to do with where we're at today?"

The sad answer is that most of the laws and regulations passed since the early part of the twentieth century are still with us. They provide both the basis for existence and the agenda for our constant companion, MAC. A great deal of this book is focused on the need to unwind, revise, or otherwise fix the financial and regulatory structures that we have inherited. As George Santayana warned, "Those who cannot remember the past are condemned to repeat it."

References

1. *Health at a Glance, OECD Indicators*, Organization for Economic Cooperation and Development, Paris, France, 2015, pp. 80–81.
2. *The Complexities of Physician Supply and Demand: Projections from 2015–2030*, The American Association of Medical Colleges, Washington, DC, 2017 Update, p. vii.

Index